DECORATING YOUR HOME FOR CHRISTMAS

104 Projects & Ideas for Christmas Decorating

The Home Decorating Institute®

Copyright © 1994 Cy DeCosse Incorporated 5900 Green Oak Drive Minnetonka, Minnesota 55343
1-800-328-3895 All rights reserved Printed in U.S.A.

Library of Congress Cataloging-in-Publication Data Decorating your home for Christmas / Home Decorating Institute. p. cm. —
(Arts & crafts for home decorating) Includes index. ISBN 0-86573-367-8 (hardcover) ISBN 0-86573-368-6 (softcover) 1. Christmas
decorations I. Home Decorating Institute (Minnetonka, Minn.) II. Series.   TT900.C4D427 1994 745.594'12—dc20   94-13145

CONTENTS

Decorating The Tree

The Holiday Table

Around The House

Gift Wrapping

DECORATING YOUR HOME FOR CHRISTMAS

Decorate for Christmas with projects that are elegant, country, or natural in style.

Each decorating style emphasizes certain elements. When decorating in a specific style, continue the look throughout a room or the entire home. Concentrate the majority of decorations in one area, such as on a Christmas tree or mantel, to create an area of emphasis. Then, place some decorations in other areas to help integrate the style.

For the Christmas tree, make a variety of trimmings suited to your personal style, including tree toppers, ornaments, garlands, and tree skirts.

To help carry a decorating style throughout your home, make coordinating table linens or a fresh floral arrangement for the dining table. Decorate a mantel with trimmed stockings and a charming elf or Father Christmas. Or create a gingerbread-style graham cracker village that will delight children and guests.

Use gift wraps that also complement your decorating style. Embellish packages with embossed cards and stamped gift-wrapping paper, selecting papers and design motifs to complement the elegant, natural, or country look of your home.

AN ELEGANT CHRISTMAS

Elegant decorating
combines rich colors
with gold accessories.

Elegant decorating is formal and sophisticated in style. Gold accessories can be used to help create an elegant setting. Use gilded ornaments and gold wired ribbon to embellish everything from trees, to garlands, to mantels, to gifts. Combining gold tones with rich jewel tones or a soft creamy white can also produce an elegant look.

Rich fabrics, such as damasks, tapestries, and velvets, are often used to make elegantly styled table linens, tree skirts, and stockings. Ornate trims and tassels can be added to accessories for additional embellishment.

Several items shown here can be made following the instructions in this book:

1. Folded star ornaments (page 33).
2. Trimmed fabric ornaments (page 36).
3. Gold-leaf ornaments (page 38).
4. Wired-ribbon garland (page 42).

5. Tree skirt (page 48).
6. Fresh floral arrangement (page 54).
7. Holiday table runner (page 61).
8. Father Christmas (page 79)
9. Gift wraps (page 120).

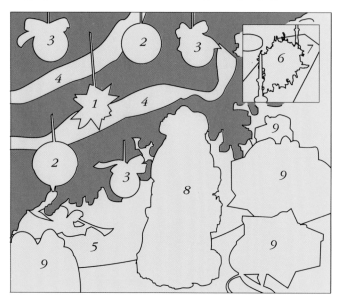

A COUNTRY
CHRISTMAS

*Country decorating
showcases handcrafted
or antique accessories.*

Country-style decorating is usually casual and informal.
Elements of this style are valued for their handcrafted,
antique, or old-fashioned appearance. Colors are soft and
subtle, sometimes with yellowed tones. Natural-fiber
fabrics are often used with this decorating style. Cotton
fabrics can be tea-dyed and frayed for a worn look.
Decorating accents made from wood can be stained
and sanded to produce an aged appearance. Christmas
gifts for a country style may be wrapped in plain brown
paper and embellished with a tea-dyed or aromatic
dough ornament.

Several items shown here can be made following the
instructions in this book:

1. *Tea-dyed ornaments
   (page 21).*
2. *Aromatic dough
   ornaments (page 26).*
3. *Quick and easy
   ornaments (page 40).*
4. *Wrapped ball-and-spool
   garland (page 42).*
5. *Tree skirt (page 48).*

6. *Pieced star table topper
   (page 69).*
7. *Father Christmas
   (page 79).*
8. *Santa's elf (page 84).*
9. *Wooden cutouts
   (page 88).*
10. *Stamped gift wrap
    (page 119).*

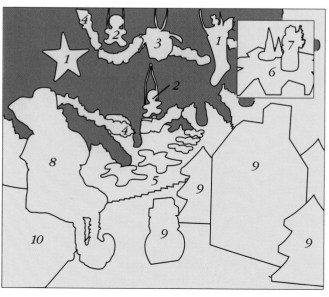

A NATURAL CHRISTMAS

*A natural-style Christmas
brings together
decorative elements from nature.*

A natural decorating style is informal and relaxed, varying
from woodsy to rustic, depending on the colors used
and the elements chosen. Natural items that help create
a natural Christmas look include items made from wood,
paper, floral materials, and spices. This style often uses
dried floral materials, such as honeysuckle vine, hydrangea,
and pepper berries for decorating trees and garlands.
Dried fruit slices and cinnamon sticks can also be used
as decorating accents. Raffia, jute, or cotton cording can
be used in place of ribbon for decorating packages.

Several items shown here can be made following the
instructions in this book:

1. *Cinnamon-stick star*
   (page 15).
2. *Spice ornaments (page 24).*
3. *Quick and easy*
   ornaments (page 40).
4. *Rope garland (page 42).*
5. *Tree skirt (page 48).*

6. *Father Christmas*
   (page 79).
7. *Embossed cards*
   (page 114).
8. *Cards and tags*
   (page 116).
9. *Gift wraps (page 120).*

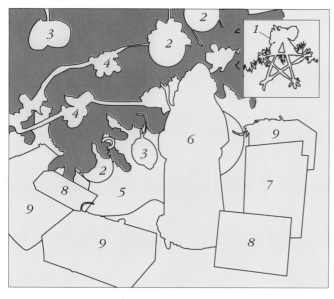

Decorating The Tree

TREE TOPPERS

A tree topper adds the finishing touch to a Christmas tree. Select one that coordinates with the style or theme of the ornaments, such as a paper-twist angel to complement a tree with a homespun look. Make a wire-mesh bow to top a tree that is decorated with glittery or metallic objects, or make a cinnamon-stick star for a tree decorated with natural ornaments.

The angel shown opposite is crafted from paper twist, a tightly wrapped paper cording that, when untwisted, produces a crinkled paper strip. The angel is given dimension with the help of wire. The outline of the wings is shaped from paper twist with a wire inner core, and the garment and shawl have craft wire encased in the fold of the hems, allowing them to be shaped into drapes and folds. Embellish the angel as desired with a miniature artificial garland or tiny musical instrument.

For an elegant-looking tree topper, create a large wire-mesh bow from aluminum window screening. The window screening, available in shiny silver and dull charcoal gray, may be left unfinished or painted gold, brass, or copper. The bow may also be sprayed with aerosol glitter for added sparkle.

For a natural look, make a star from cinnamon sticks held together with hot glue and raffia. The star can be embellished with a raffia bow, miniature cones, and a few sprigs of greenery.

Angel *(opposite) is created from paper twist, sinamay ribbon, jute, and raffia, for a country look.*

Wire-mesh bow, *created from window screening, is sprayed with gold metallic paint for an elegant look.*

Cinnamon-stick star *is embellished with sprigs of greenery, red raffia, and miniature cones.*

MATERIALS

- Poster board.
- Packing tape.
- Three 1½" (3.8 cm) Styrofoam® balls.
- ½ yd. (0.5 m) paper twist, 4" to 4½" (10 to 11.5 cm) wide, in skintone or natural color, for head, neck, and hands.
- 1 yd. (0.95 m) paper twist, 4" to 4½" (10 to 11.5 cm) wide, for shawl.
- 2 yd. (1.85 m) paper twist, 7" to 7½" (18 to 19.3 cm) wide, for dress.

- 1 yd. (0.95 m) paper twist with wire inner core, for wings.
- Sinamay ribbon, at least 2" (5 cm) wide, for wings.
- Raffia.
- 3-ply jute.
- Dowel, ⅛" (3 mm) in diameter.
- 24-gauge craft wire.
- Thick craft glue.
- Hot glue gun and glue sticks.
- Wire cutter or utility scissors.
- Miniature garland or other desired embellishments.

CUTTING DIRECTIONS

From skintone or natural paper twist, cut one 4" (10 cm) piece for the head, one 10" (25 cm) piece for the underbodice, and three ¾" (2 cm) pieces for the neck and hands.

From the paper twist for the dress, cut two 4½" (11.5 cm) pieces for the sleeves, six 8½" (21.8 cm) pieces for the skirt, and one 7" (18 cm) piece for the dress bodice.

From the paper twist with a wire inner core, cut one 12" (30.5 cm) length for the arms and one 24" (61 cm) length for the wings.

1 Cut a semicircle with 8" (20.5 cm) radius from poster board. Trim 6" (15 cm) pie-shaped wedge from one end; discard. Form cone with base 15" (38 cm) in diameter; secure with packing tape. Press the Styrofoam balls between fingers to compress to 1¼" (3.2 cm) in diameter.

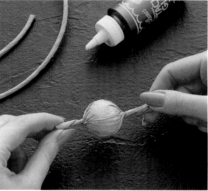

2 Untwist paper twist for head; glue width of paper around Styrofoam ball, using craft glue. Apply craft glue to ball at top and bottom, and tightly retwist paper; apply additional glue as necessary so paper stays twisted. Allow glue to dry.

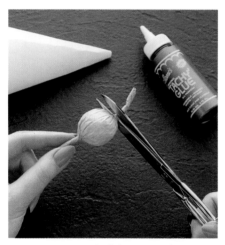

3 Trim one end of the twisted paper close to foam ball; this will be top of head. Poke remaining twisted end into top of cone; trim top of cone, if necessary. Remove head, and set aside.

4 Poke a hole through each side of the cone, 1" (2.5 cm) from top; for the arms, insert the paper twist with the wire inner core through the holes. Push each wire arm through the center of Styrofoam ball; for shoulders, slide balls up to the cone. Shape balls to fit snugly against cone by pressing with fingers; secure to cone with hot glue, applying the glue to the cone.

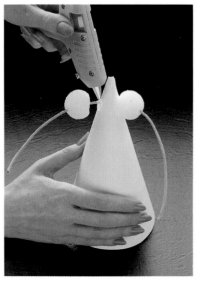

5 Bend each wire arm 1" (2.5 cm) from end; bend to form triangle shape for hands. Untwist a paper strip for hand; mist it with water. Wrap paper around the hand; secure with craft glue. Repeat for the other hand. Untwist and mist the paper strip for neck. Wrap paper around top of cone; secure with craft glue.

6 Untwist underbodice piece; cut a small slit in center. Position slit in paper over top of cone; smooth paper around shoulders and cone. Secure with craft glue. Glue head in place.

7 Untwist skirt pieces. Join the skirt pieces together by overlapping long edges ¼" (6 mm); secure with glue to form tube. Fold ½" (1.3 cm) hem on one edge; insert wire into fold, overlapping ends of wire about 1" (2.5 cm). Secure hem with craft glue, encasing wire.

8 Place cone on a soup or vegetable can. Slide skirt over cone, with the hem about 2" (5 cm) below the lower edge of the cone. Hand-gather upper edge to fit smoothly around the waist; secure with wire. Shape wired hem into graceful folds.

9 Untwist sleeve piece. Overlap the edges ¼" (6 mm) to form a tube; secure with craft glue. Fold the hem, encasing the wire as in step 7. Slide sleeve over arm, placing hem at wrist. Glue sleeve at shoulder, sides, and underarm, concealing underbodice at underarm. Shape wired hem. Repeat for other sleeve.

10 Untwist dress bodice piece; cut in half lengthwise. Fold strips in half lengthwise. Drape one strip over each shoulder, placing folded edges at neck; cross the ends at front and back; glue in place. Wrap wire around waist; trim excess.

11 Cut several lengths of raffia, about 25" (63.5 cm) long; mist with water. Tie raffia around waist, concealing the wire; trim ends. Cut thicker raffia lengths, and separate into two or three strands.

12 Bend the paper twist with wire inner core for wings as shown; allow the ends to extend 1" (2.5 cm) beyond center. Wrap ends around center; secure with glue.

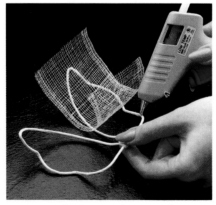

13 Bend edges and curve of wings as shown. Glue sinamay ribbon to back of wings, using hot glue. Allow glue to dry; trim away excess ribbon.

14 Position wings on back of angel at center, so wings curve away from back; secure, using hot glue.

(Continued)

15 Cut jute, and separate to make three single-ply 30" (76 cm) lengths. Wrap each ply tightly and evenly around dowel, securing the ends. Saturate jute with water. Place the dowel in 200°F (95°C) oven for 2 hours or until dry.

16 Remove jute from the dowel. Cut and glue individual lengths of coiled jute to head for hair, working in sections; for the bangs, glue short pieces across the front of the head.

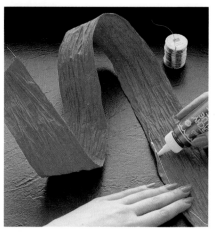

17 Untwist the shawl piece. Fold ½" (1.3 cm) hem on one long edge. Insert wire into fold; glue hem in place, encasing wire. Repeat on opposite side.

18 Drape shawl around the shoulders. Shape the wired hems to make a graceful drape; adjust the shawl in back to conceal the lower portion of the wings. Fold ends of shawl to underside of the skirt. Glue shawl in place in several areas, using hot glue.

19 Shape the wire arms to hold desired accessories. Secure any other embellishments to angel as desired, using hot glue.

HOW TO MAKE A WIRE-MESH BOW TREE TOPPER

MATERIALS

- Aluminum window screening.
- 24-gauge or 26-gauge craft wire.
- Utility scissors.
- Aerosol acrylic paint in metallic finish, optional.
- Aerosol glitter, optional.

CUTTING DIRECTIONS

Cut the following rectangles from window screening, cutting along the mesh weave: one 8" × 38" (20.5 × 96.5 cm) piece for the loops, one 8" × 28" (20.5 × 71 cm) piece for the streamers, and one 2½" × 7" (6.5 × 18 cm) rectangle for the center strip.

1 Paint both sides of each rectangle, if desired; allow to dry. Fold up ½" (1.3 cm) on long edges, using a straightedge as a guide. Fold up ½" (1.3 cm) along short edges of streamers and one short edge of center strip.

2 Cut 16" (40.5 cm) length of wire. Form a loop from rectangle for loops, overlapping the short ends about ¾" (2 cm) at center. Insert wire at one overlapped edge; twist wire to secure, leaving 2" (5 cm) tail.

3 Stitch through the center of overlapped mesh with long end of wire, taking 1" to 1½" (2.5 to 3.8 cm) stitches. Pull up wire firmly to gather mesh; wrap wire around center, and twist the ends together; trim the excess.

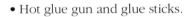

4 Hand-pleat width of streamer at the center; place below the gathered loop. Wrap length of wire around the center of loop and streamers; twist ends together. Paint wire to match bow, if necessary.

5 Wrap center strip around the bow, concealing the wire. Stitch ends together with length of wire. Apply aerosol glitter, if desired. Secure a length of wire to the back of center strip for securing bow to tree.

HOW TO MAKE A CINNAMON-STICK STAR TREE TOPPER

MATERIALS

- Five 12" (30.5 cm) cinnamon sticks.
- Hot glue gun and glue sticks.
- Raffia.
- Embellishments, such as cones and sprigs of greenery.

1 Arrange two cinnamon sticks in an "X"; position a third stick across the top, placing one end below upper stick of "X" as shown.

2 Place remaining two sticks on top in an inverted "V." Adjust spacing of cinnamon sticks as necessary, to form star. Secure sticks at ends, using hot glue.

3 Tie raffia securely around ends at intersection of cinnamon sticks. Tie several lengths of raffia into bow; glue to top of star. Secure embellishments with glue.

TEA-DYED ORNAMENTS

Add an old-fashioned, homespun look to a Christmas tree with a variety of stitch-and-turn ornaments, such as stockings, stars, trees, and snowmen. Embellish the ornaments to make each one unique.

For an aged appearance, make the ornaments from cotton quilting fabrics, and tea dye the fabrics before cutting the ornaments. Tea dying works well on light-colored fabrics. The color change will vary with the type of tea used. Orange tea, for example, gives a yellowed look to fabrics, while cranberry tea produces a reddish appearance. The amount of color change will depend on the concentration of tea used and the length of time the fabric is soaked.

MATERIALS

- Scraps of cotton quilting fabrics, such as muslin, calico, and ticking.
- Polyester fiberfill.
- Embellishments, such as buttons, cinnamon sticks, artificial or preserved greenery, and artificial berries.
- 9" (23 cm) length of cording for hanger of each snowman, star, and tree ornament.
- Large-eyed needle.
- Small twigs and round toothpick, for snowman ornament.
- Orange acrylic paint and black acrylic paint or fine-point permanent-ink marker, for details of snowman ornament.
- Drapery weight or marble, for stocking ornament.
- Hot glue gun and glue sticks.

CUTTING DIRECTIONS

Transfer the ornament pattern pieces (page 122) onto paper. For a star or stocking ornament, cut two pieces from fabric, right sides together. For a snowman or tree ornament, cut two pieces from fabric, placing the dotted line of the pattern on the fold of the fabric. For the snowman, also cut one hat piece, placing the dotted line of the pattern on the fold of the fabric.

HOW TO TEA DYE FABRIC

1 Prewash the fabric to remove any finishes. Brew strong tea, about four tea bags per 1 qt. (1 L) of water; leave tea bags in water. Soak fabric in tea until desired color is achieved; areas with air pockets will not dye as dark, and areas of fabric touching tea bags will be darker.

2 Remove fabric from the tea, and squeeze out excess; do not rinse fabric. Place the fabric on paper towel; allow to dry. Press fabric to heat-set color; use scrap of fabric to protect ironing surface from any excess tea.

HOW TO MAKE A STOCKING ORNAMENT

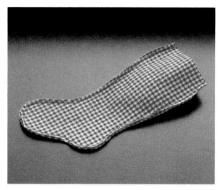

1 Place stocking pieces right sides together. Stitch ⅛" (3 mm) seam around stocking, using short stitch length: leave top open.

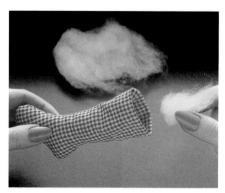

2 Turn stocking right side out; press. Fold fabric to inside along dotted line; press. Placing drapery weight or marble into toe of stocking, loosely stuff stocking with polyester fiberfill.

3 Tear ½" × 6" (1.3 × 15 cm) strip of fabric for hanger; fold strip in half. Place folded strip at top of stocking; secure by stitching a button to strip, ⅜" (1 cm) from the ends, through all layers. Secure embellishments inside stocking, using hot glue.

HOW TO MAKE A STAR ORNAMENT

1 Cut a ¾" (2 cm) slit through center of one star piece. Place the pieces right sides together; stitch ⅛" (3 mm) seam around star, using a short stitch length. Trim off the points, and clip the inner corners.

2 Turn star right side out through the slit; stuff star firmly with polyester fiberfill. Hand-stitch opening closed, and take two or three stitches through center of star; pull stitches to indent center. Secure thread.

3 Glue embellishments to star over stitched opening in center. Thread cord for hanger through the needle; take a stitch through star at desired location. Knot ends of cord together.

HOW TO MAKE A TREE ORNAMENT

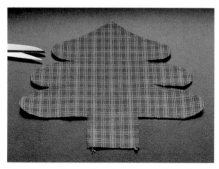

1 Place pieces for the tree right sides together. Stitch ⅛" (3 mm) seam around the tree, using a short stitch length; leave opening on lower edge of trunk. Clip corners and curves.

2 Turn tree right side out. Stuff tree with polyester fiberfill, stuffing branches first.

3 Turn raw edges to inside on lower edge of trunk; slipstitch closed. Stitch or glue buttons to the ends of the branches. Secure the hanger as in step 3, above.

HOW TO MAKE A SNOWMAN ORNAMENT

1 Place snowman pieces right sides together. Stitch ⅛" (3 mm) seam around the snowman, using short stitch length; leave a 1" (2.5 cm) opening at top. Clip seam allowances as necessary. Fold hat in half, right sides together, matching raw edges; stitch ⅛" (3 mm) seam on the edge opposite fold.

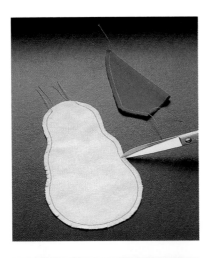

2 Turn snowman right side out; stuff firmly with polyester fiberfill. Turn raw edges to inside on upper edge; slipstitch opening closed.

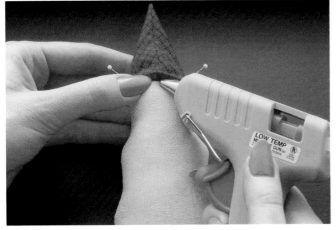

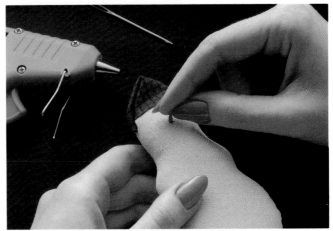

3 Turn hat right side out; fold fabric to inside along dotted line. Position hat on snowman with seam at center back; secure with hot glue. Fold the peak of the hat over to one side; secure with a dot of hot glue.

4 Break off ½" (1.3 cm) from round toothpick for nose; paint nose orange. Using a large-eyed needle, poke hole in fabric at desired location for nose. Apply a dot of hot glue to blunt end of nose; insert in hole.

5 Make dots for eyes and mouth, using acrylic paint or a fine-point permanent-ink marker. Tear ½" × 8" (1.3 × 20.5 cm) fabric strip for scarf; tie scarf around neck of snowman.

6 Poke holes in fabric on each side of snowman at the desired location for twig arms; apply glue to end of each twig and insert into the holes. Secure any embellishments with hot glue. Secure cord for hanger as in step 3 for star, opposite.

SPICE ORNAMENTS

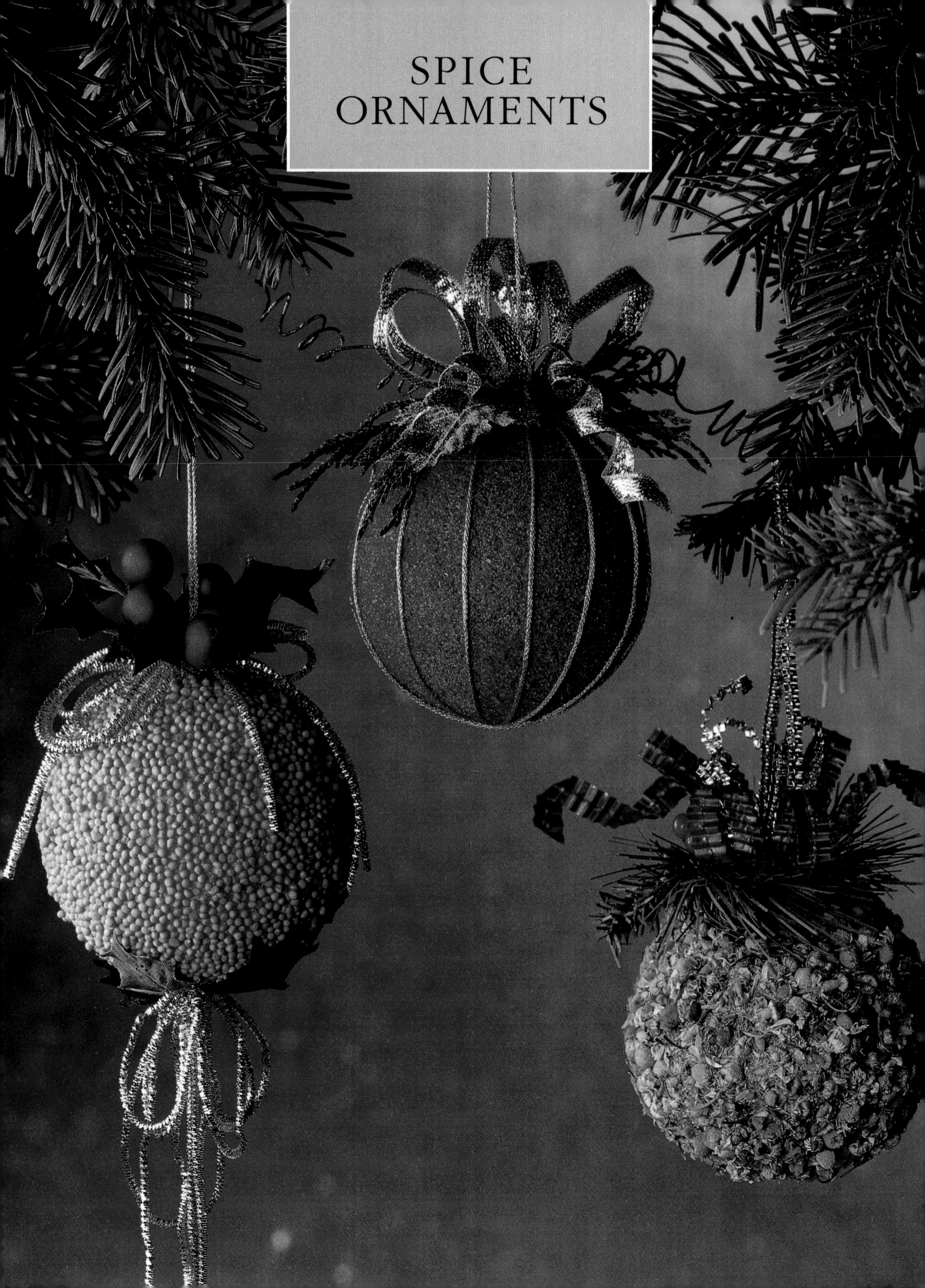

Spice ornaments are fragrant and colorful additions to the holiday tree. They are made by covering Styrofoam® balls with powdered or crushed dried spices. To create a variety of looks, the simple ornaments can be embellished with ribbons and preserved or artificial leaves or berries. For durability, the spice-covered ornaments are sprayed with an aerosol clear acrylic sealer.

MATERIALS

- Powdered or crushed dried spices, such as nutmeg, cinnamon, oregano, mace, paprika, parsley, poppy seed, crushed red pepper, allspice, mustard seed, chili powder, or dried orange peel.
- Aerosol acrylic paints in colors that blend with spices.
- Styrofoam balls.
- 20-gauge craft wire.
- 9" (23 cm) length of ribbon or cording, for hanger.
- Thick craft glue; hot glue gun and glue sticks.
- Aerosol clear acrylic sealer.
- Embellishments as desired.

Spice ornaments, arranged in a bowl, are made with paprika, crushed red pepper, mace, allspice, mustard seed, cinnamon, and chili powder.

HOW TO MAKE A SPICE ORNAMENT

1 Roll Styrofoam ball lightly against table to compress the Styrofoam slightly.

2 Spray Styrofoam ball with aerosol acrylic paint; allow to dry.

3 Apply craft glue to the Styrofoam ball; roll in spice to cover. Allow to dry. Apply aerosol acrylic sealer.

4 Knot the ends of the ribbon or cording together. Bend 4" (10 cm) length of wire in half. Attach ribbon or cording to the ornament with wire as shown; secure with dot of hot glue.

5 Secure any additional embellishments to the ornament as desired, using hot glue.

AROMATIC DOUGH ORNAMENTS

For an old-fashioned country look, you can decorate the Christmas tree with aromatic dough ornaments. A variety of ornaments can be created, depending on the shapes of cookie cutters used. Either a microwave or a conventional oven can be used for making the ornaments. The conventional oven method may produce ornaments with a more irregular surface. The microwave directions are based on a 600-watt microwave oven. The cooking time and finished product may vary, depending on the wattage and size of your microwave oven.

For added embellishment, decorate the ornaments with whole cloves, allspice, cinnamon candies, or bits of dough. Hang the ornaments from the tree with ribbon, raffia, or torn strips of cotton fabric.

MATERIALS

- Ingredients for aromatic dough, opposite.
- Mixing bowl; floured board; rolling pin; cookie cutters.
- 10" (25.5 cm) pie plate for microwave method, or baking sheet for conventional oven method.
- Garlic press, optional.
- Drinking straw, ⅜" (1 cm) in diameter.
- Nonstick vegetable cooking spray.
- 9" (23 cm) length of ribbon or raffia, for hanger.
- Embellishments, such as cinnamon candies, whole cloves, or allspice.

HOW TO MAKE AROMATIC DOUGH ORNAMENTS

1 Prepare aromatic dough (left). Roll dough to ¼" (6 mm) thickness on lightly floured surface; work with small portions of the dough at a time. Cut out the shapes with cookie cutters.

2 Embellish cutouts with cinnamon candies, cloves, allspice, or bits of textured dough; make the textured dough by pushing small amounts of dough through a garlic press. Secure the dough to cutouts by moistening it with water. Cut hole for hanger near top of cutout, using drinking straw.

3 Spray pie plate or baking sheet with vegetable cooking spray. Place cutouts on prepared pie plate or baking sheet. Microwave or bake in conventional oven as directed below. **Microwave oven method.** Cook at 30% (Medium Low) for 5 to 8 minutes, or until the tops of the cutouts feel dry, rotating the plate and checking the ornaments every 2 minutes. **Conventional oven method.** Bake for about 2 hours, or until tops are dry and feel firm to the touch.

4 Remove ornaments to a rack and set aside for 24 hours or longer to complete drying. If desired, spray the ornaments lightly with vegetable cooking spray for glossier appearance. Insert the ribbon or raffia for hangers through the holes of the ornaments; knot ends together.

Note: These ornaments are for decoration only.

METAL ORNAMENTS

Metal ornaments made from either copper or tin add a whimsical look to a tree. The metals are available at craft stores in sheets of various sizes. Copper is the thinner of the two and cuts easily with household utility scissors; tin can be cut best with a jeweler's snips, available at jewelry-making supply stores. Both metals are suitable for flat ornaments; however, tin can also be used to make spiral ornaments. To create chained ornaments, two or more ornaments can be wired together.

Metal ornaments can be embellished, if desired, with craft wire or a punched design. Simple shapes for the ornaments and the punched designs can be found on gift-wrapping paper, greeting cards, and cookie cutters.

You may enlarge or reduce simple designs on a photocopy machine, if desired.

For a country or rustic look, copper can easily be given a weathered or aged appearance through a process called oxidizing. Heat oxidizing is done by placing the copper ornament over a flame until the color changes. The copper ornament is moved randomly over the flame to produce uneven coloring. A gas stove works well for oxidizing copper, because it produces a clean flame. Hold the copper with tongs while heating, because the metal becomes very hot. For additional texture, sand the surface of the copper before it is heated, using medium-grit sandpaper.

MATERIALS

- Copper or tin sheet.
- Awl and rubber mallet, or tin-punching tool.
- Utility scissors or jeweler's snips.
- Scrap of wood.
- Tracing paper and transfer paper.
- Masking tape.

- 22-gauge to 28-gauge brass or copper craft wire.
- Fine steel wool.
- 100-grit sandpaper.
- Tongs with handles that do not conduct heat, for oxidizing copper.
- Aerosol clear acrylic sealer.

HOW TO MAKE A COPPER OR TIN FLAT ORNAMENT

1 Cover the work surface with a newspaper. Transfer the desired design for the ornament onto tracing paper. Transfer design to metal sheet, using transfer paper.

2 Place ornament design over scrap of wood. Punch hole for hanger about ⅛" (3 mm) inside edge of design, using an awl and mallet. Embellish interior of ornament with a punched design, if desired (page 31).

(Continued)

3 Cut out ornament, using scissors or jeweler's snips. Trim the tips off any sharp points.

4 Sand edges of ornament lightly, using sandpaper to smooth any sharp edges of metal; avoid sanding surface of ornament if smooth finish is desired.

5 Rub the ornament with fine steel wool to remove any fingerprints. Oxidize copper, if desired (opposite). Spray with aerosol clear acrylic sealer.

6 Embellish the ornament, if desired, by wrapping it with wire; for additional textural interest, layer two ornaments, then wrap with wire. Twist ends of wire together on back side; trim off excess.

7 Cut 7" (18 cm) length of wire, for hanger. Twist end of wire around awl, to make a coil, as in step 1, opposite. Insert opposite end of wire through the hole from the front of ornament; bend end to make hook for hanging.

HOW TO MAKE A TIN SPIRAL ORNAMENT

1 Cut ¼" × 6" (6 mm × 15 cm) strip of tin; trim ends at an angle. Trim off any sharp points, using jeweler's snips. Sand edges lightly with sandpaper. Punch a hole for hanger about ⅛" (3 mm) from one end of the strip, using an awl and mallet.

2 Wrap tin strip around pencil to make spiral; remove ornament from the pencil. Spray with aerosol clear acrylic sealer. Add hanger as in step 7, above.

HOW TO CONNECT METAL ORNAMENTS WITH WIRE

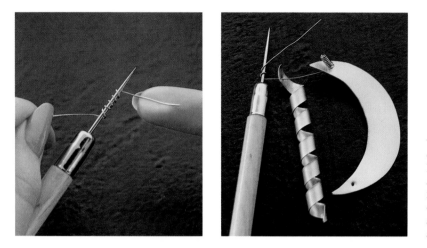

1 Cut 6" (15 cm) length of wire. Twist end of wire around awl to make a coil, using about 2¼" (6 cm) of wire. Press coil together between fingers to compress slightly.

2 Insert opposite end of the wire through hole in one ornament from front. Insert wire through second ornament from back. Repeat coiling process to secure the wire to second ornament.

HOW TO PUNCH A DESIGN IN A METAL ORNAMENT

1 Transfer the design for punching to tissue paper as on page 29, step 1. Tape the design for punching to metal sheet inside lines for ornament.

2 Punch holes around the edges of design at ⅛" (3 mm) intervals, using awl and mallet. Remove tissue pattern.

HOW TO OXIDIZE COPPER

1 Texturize copper sheet, if desired, by sanding lightly with sandpaper.

2 Hold the copper ornament over flame with tongs; move it through flame randomly to produce color change. Remove the ornament from heat occasionally to check for desired color; holding the copper in flame too long can cause the copper to lose all its natural color.

FOLDED STAR ORNAMENTS

Using simple folding techniques, turn strips of paper or ribbon into delicate and dimensional folded star ornaments, sometimes called German stars. Each star ornament is made from only four strips of paper or ribbon. The width of the paper strips or ribbon determines the size of the ornament. Use the chart at right to help determine the width and length of the strips needed to make a folded star ornament of the desired size.

For folded star ornaments from paper, select papers of medium weight, such as parchment papers and gift-wrapping papers. Many art supply stores have large sheets of decorative papers with unique textures. To make gift-wrapping paper decorative on both sides, you can fuse two sheets together, using lightweight paper-backed fusible web. Test-fuse small pieces of paper to be sure the paper does not become too stiff to crease easily.

For folded star ornaments made from ribbon, select ribbons that are attractive on both sides and that hold a crease well, such as some craft and metallic ribbons; avoid satin or taffeta ribbons.

CUTTING DIRECTIONS

For each folded star ornament from paper, cut four strips of paper, using the chart below as a guide for determining the width and length of the strips.

For a folded star ornament from ribbon, cut four lengths of ribbon, using the chart below as a guide for determining the length of the strips; the length depends on the width of the ribbon used.

MATERIALS

- Paper or ribbon, amount depending on size of star desired.
- Lightweight paper-backed fusible web, for use with papers that are decorative on one side only.
- Thick craft glue; decorative thread or cording, for hanger.

SIZE CHART FOR FOLDED STAR ORNAMENTS

APPROXIMATE SIZE	WIDTH OF STRIP	LENGTH OF STRIP	RIBBON YARDAGE REQUIRED
2" (5 cm)	½" (1.3 cm)	15" (38 cm)	1¾ yd. (1.6 m)
3" to 3½" (7.5 to 9 cm)	⅝" to ¾" (1.5 to 2 cm)	18" (46 cm)	2 yd. (1.85 m)
4½" (11.5 cm)	1" (2.5 cm)	27" (68.5 cm)	3 yd. (2.75 m)
6½" to 7" (16.3 to 18 cm)	1⅜" to 1½" (3.5 to 3.8 cm)	36" (91.5 cm)	4 yd. (3.7 m)
9" (23 cm)	2" (5 cm)	46" (117 cm)	5⅛ yd. (4.7 m)

HOW TO FUSE PAPER

1 Fuse adhesive side of paper-backed fusible web to the wrong side of decorative paper, using dry iron set at medium temperature; press for 1 to 3 seconds. Remove paper backing; set aside to use as press cloth.

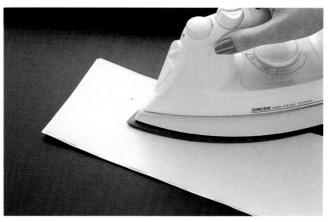

2 Place second sheet of paper over the first piece, with wrong sides together. Using paper backing as a press cloth, fuse layers together for 1 to 3 seconds.

HOW TO MAKE A FOLDED STAR ORNAMENT

1 Fold each of the four strips in half; trim ends to points. Place two folded strips vertically, with the tips of the left strip pointing up and tips of right strip pointing down.

2 Place the left vertical strip between layers of a third strip, positioning it near fold of third strip. Place ends of third strip between the layers of the right vertical strip.

3 Weave the fourth strip below third strip by placing ends of right vertical strip between layers of fourth strip. Place ends of fourth strip between layers of left vertical strip. Pull ends tightly.

4 Fold top layer of left vertical strip down; crease. Rotate woven square one-quarter turn clockwise.

5 Repeat step 4 to fold the next two top layers down; insert fourth strip between layers of the lower left square as shown. Crease and rotate one-quarter turn clockwise.

6 Fold upper right strip over itself at 45° angle as shown; crease.

7 Fold same strip over itself at 45° angle as shown; crease.

8 Fold same strip to left, aligning folded edges; insert end of strip between layers of upper right square to make one star point. Rotate woven square one-quarter turn clockwise.

9 Repeat steps 6 to 8 to make four star points.

10 Turn star over. Repeat steps 6 to 8 to make four more star points, for a total of eight star points.

11 Lift horizontal strip at upper right corner to the left, out of the way. Fold up vertical strip at lower right; crease.

12 Fold same strip over itself at 45° angle as shown; crease. Grasp end of strip; keep this side of the strip facing up as you complete step 13.

13 Turn the strip counterclockwise; insert end of strip between layers of upper left square. Strip will come out through star point; open point of star with finger or tip of scissors, if necessary. Pull tight to make star point that projects upward.

14 Rotate star one-quarter turn clockwise and repeat steps 11 to 13 to make four projecting star points.

15 Turn star over. Repeat steps 11 to 14 to make four additional projecting star points. Trim ends of strips even with edge of outer star points. Secure by applying dot of glue to both sides of ends, if necessary.

16 Thread needle; insert needle through star between two outer points. Knot ends of thread for hanger.

TRIMMED FABRIC ORNAMENTS

Create elegant ornaments by covering Styrofoam® balls with rich fabrics and trims. Four wedge-shaped fabric pieces are used to cover the Styrofoam ball. Use one fabric, or select up to four different coordinating fabrics, to cover the ball. The fabric pieces are glued to the ball, and the raw edges are concealed with flat trim, such as ribbon or braid. Cording, pearls, sequins, or beads can also be used to embellish the ornament. The hanger of the ornament is made from a decorative cord and an ornamental cap.

MATERIALS

- 3" (7.5 cm) Styrofoam ball.
- Fabric scraps.
- Cording and flat trims, such as ribbon or braid.
- Decorative beads, pearls, sequins, and bead pins, optional.
- 9" (23 cm) length of cording and ornamental cap, for hanger.
- Thick craft glue; hot glue gun and glue sticks.

HOW TO MAKE A TRIMMED FABRIC ORNAMENT

1 Transfer the pattern (page 124) to paper, and cut four pieces from fabric scraps.

2 Apply craft glue near the edges on the wrong side of one fabric piece. Position the fabric piece on Styrofoam ball; smooth edges around the ball, easing fullness along sides.

3 Apply remaining fabric pieces to ball; match points and align raw edges to cover ball completely.

4 Glue trim over the raw edges of the fabric pieces, butting raw edges of trim at top of ornament.

5 Poke hole in Styrofoam ball at top of ornament. Insert end of one or two pieces of cording into hole; secure with craft glue. Apply glue to fabric as shown; wrap the cording tightly around the ball in one continuous spiral, until desired effect is achieved. Poke end of cording into Styrofoam; secure with glue.

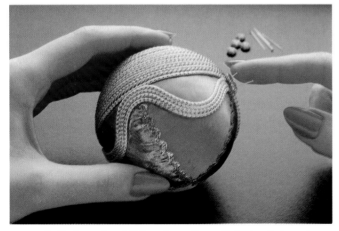

6 Embellish with additional cording, if desired. Attach decorative beads, pearls, and sequins, if desired, using bead pins; secure with dot of craft glue.

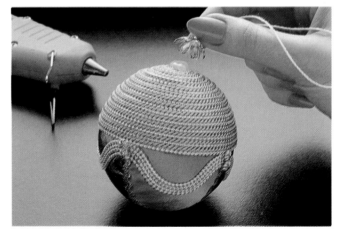

7 Insert cord in decorative cap; knot ends. Shape cap to fit top of ornament; secure with hot glue. Add bead or decorative cap to bottom, if desired.

GOLD-LEAF ORNAMENTS

Turn papier-mâché craft ornaments into elegant gold-leaf ornaments, using imitation gold leaf.

Imitation leaf, also available in silver and copper, can be found at craft and art supply stores. Several sheets are packaged together, with tissue paper between the layers. When working with the sheets of gold leaf, handle the tissue paper, not the gold leaf, whenever possible. The gold leaf is very fragile and may tarnish.

MATERIALS

- Papier-mâché ball.
- Aerosol acrylic paint, optional.
- Imitation gold, silver, or copper leaf.
- Gold-leaf adhesive; paintbrush.
- Soft-bristle brush.
- Ribbon, for bow.
- Thick craft glue; aerosol clear acrylic sealer.

HOW TO MAKE A GOLD-LEAF ORNAMENT

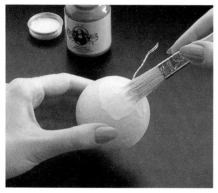

1 Apply aerosol paint to the papier-mâché ball, if desired; allow paint to dry. Apply gold-leaf adhesive to the ornament in small area, feathering out edges; allow the adhesive to dry until clear.

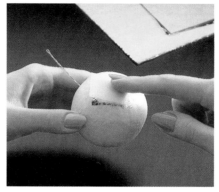

2 Cut the gold leaf and tissue paper slightly larger than adhesive area. Press the gold leaf over the adhesive, handling the tissue only. Remove the tissue paper.

3 Remove excess gold leaf with a soft-bristle brush. Apply gold leaf to additional areas of ball as desired. Apply aerosol clear acrylic sealer. Tie ribbon in bow around base of hanger; secure with dot of craft glue.

MARBLEIZED ORNAMENTS

Elegant marbleized ornaments are easy to make, using clear glass ornaments and craft acrylic paints. For best results, use paints that are of pouring consistency; paints may be thinned with water, if necessary. The marbleized effect is created by pouring two or three colors of paint into a glass ornament and swirling the paint colors together. Allow the paints to dry slightly after each color is applied, to avoid a muddy appearance.

MATERIALS

- Clear glass ornament, with removable top.
- Craft acrylic paints in desired colors.
- 9" (23 cm) length of cording or ribbon, for hanger.
- Ribbon, for bow.
- Disposable cups; hot glue gun and glue sticks.

HOW TO MAKE A MARBLEIZED ORNAMENT

1 Remove cap from ornament. Pour first color of paint into disposable cup; thin with water, if necessary. Pour small amount of paint into ornament; rotate to swirl paint. Place ornament, upside down, on the cup; allow any excess paint to flow out.

2 Repeat step 1 for each remaining color of paint. Place the ornament, upside down, on a cup, and allow the excess paint to flow out. Turn ornament right side up; allow to dry. Paint colors will continue to mix together during the drying process. Use additional coats of paint as necessary for opaque appearance.

3 Replace cap on ornament. Insert cording or ribbon through wire loop in cap; knot ends. Make a bow from ribbon; secure to top of ornament, using hot glue.

QUICK & EASY ORNAMENTS

Wheat bundles (left), hung upside down, are attractive accents on trees with natural or country decorating styles. The wheat stems are secured in bundles with a rubber band, which is concealed with a fabric bow. Secure the ornaments to the tree using floral wire.

Wire garland, shaped into spirals, adds glitz to a Christmas tree. Wrap a 26" (66 cm) length of wire garland around a pen or pencil. Remove the wire, then gradually untwist the coil from one end to make the ornament. At the widest end, bend the wire to form a hanger.

Glitter adds sparkle to plain ornaments. Mark designs on the ornaments using a glue-stick pen, then sprinkle with extra-fine glitter.

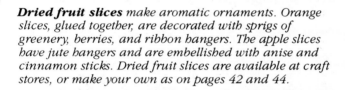

Dried fruit slices make aromatic ornaments. Orange slices, glued together, are decorated with sprigs of greenery, berries, and ribbon hangers. The apple slices have jute hangers and are embellished with anise and cinnamon sticks. Dried fruit slices are available at craft stores, or make your own as on pages 42 and 44.

Torn fabric strips are wrapped and glued around Styrofoam® balls to make country-style ornaments. Secure raffia bows and hangers with hot glue.

Ribbons and berries embellish the tops of purchased glass ornaments. Ribbons also replace the traditional wire hangers.

Glitter glue in fine-tip tubes is applied to a glass ball ornament, creating a unique dimensional design.

GARLANDS

Tree garlands can be made in a variety of styles. Shown top to bottom, choose from a rope garland, wrapped ball-and-spool garland, a dried-fruit-slice garland, or a wired-ribbon garland.

For ease in assembling, make the garlands in lengths of about 72" (183 cm). The wired-ribbon garland can be made any length. Most garlands are constructed with loops at the ends for securing the garlands to the branches.

Decorate a tree with a country or natural look, using a rope garland embellished with berry or floral clusters. The clusters may be purchased ready-made, or you can make your own.

To make a wrapped ball-and-spool garland with a country look, wrap torn fabric strips around Styrofoam® balls and wooden spools, then string them together with a piece of jute or twine. Buttons can be added to the garland for more color. Adding buttons decreases the number of wrapped balls and spools needed.

For a dried-fruit-slice garland, combine dried apple and orange slices with cinnamon sticks and fresh cranberries. String the items together with a piece of raffia for a natural look. You can dry your own fruit slices by placing them in a low-temperature oven for several hours. The drying time will vary, depending on the moisture content of the fruit. Remove the fruit slices from the oven when they feel like leather. If the slices are dried too long, they will be brittle and break; if the drying time is too short, they will be soft and spoil. The fresh cranberries will dry naturally on the garland after it is made.

A wired-ribbon garland can be made inexpensively from fabric strips, beading wire, and paper-backed fusible web. Decorate a tree with one continuous garland or several shorter ones. Arrange the garland by weaving the ribbon between and into the branches to create depth.

HOW TO MAKE A ROPE GARLAND

MATERIALS

- 1⅓ yd. (1.27 m) two-ply or three-ply manila or sisal rope, ¼" or ⅜" (6 mm or 1 cm) in diameter.
- Sheet moss.
- Eight berry or floral clusters with wire stems, either purchased or made as on page 100.
- Wire cutter.
- Hot glue gun and glue sticks; thick craft glue.

1 Make 3" (7.5 cm) loops at ends of rope by inserting each end between plies; secure with hot glue.

2 Make eight berry or floral clusters, if necessary (page 100). Insert the wire stems of clusters between the plies of rope at 8" (20.5 cm) intervals, and secure them with hot glue; trim any excess wire, using wire cutter.

3 Conceal wire ends of clusters with pieces of sheet moss; secure with craft glue.

HOW TO MAKE A WRAPPED BALL-AND-SPOOL GARLAND

MATERIALS

- Scraps of cotton fabrics.
- Twenty-four ⅞" (2.2 cm) Styrofoam® balls.
- Twenty-four wooden craft spools.
- Assorted buttons, optional.
- Lightweight jute or twine.
- Large-eyed needle.
- Thick craft glue.

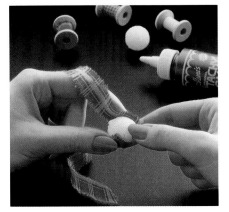

1 Tear twenty-four ¾" × 2¼" (2 × 6 cm) fabric strips on crosswise grain. Wrap around wooden spools; secure with glue. Tear twenty-four ½" × 13" (1.3 × 33 cm) fabric strips. Wrap randomly around Styrofoam balls; secure with glue.

2 Cut an 84" (213.5 cm) length of jute or twine. Form 3" (7.5 cm) loop at one end, and secure with knot; thread a large-eyed needle on opposite end.

3 String wrapped balls and spools onto jute or twine, alternating with buttons, if desired. Form loop at end; secure with knot.

HOW TO MAKE A DRIED-FRUIT-SLICE GARLAND

MATERIALS

- Firm apples and oranges.
- Fresh cranberries.
- Cinnamon sticks.

- 2 cups (500 mL) lemon juice.
- 1 tablespoon (15 mL) salt.

- Parchment paper.
- Raffia.
- 24-gauge floral wire.

- Wire cutter.
- Aerosol clear acrylic sealer.
- Paper towels.

1 Mix lemon and salt together; set aside. Cut fruit into scant ¼" (6 mm) slices, cutting crosswise as shown. Soak apple slices in lemon solution for 1 minute. Pat slices with paper towels to absorb excess moisture.

2 Place apple and orange slices on cookie sheet lined with parchment paper. Bake in 150°F (65°C) oven for 8 to 12 hours, until slices are dry, but still pliable; turn slices over and open oven door periodically while drying.

3 Apply aerosol clear acrylic sealer to cooled fruit slices. Break cinnamon sticks into 2" (5 cm) lengths. Select length of sturdy raffia; form loop at one end, and secure with knot.

4 Create needle for stringing fruit by folding a 6" (15 cm) length of floral wire in half around the unknotted end of raffia. Twist wire together at ends; trim excess, using wire cutter. Crimp the wire at fold, using pliers.

5 String the fruit slices, cranberries, and cinnamon sticks onto raffia; pierce fruit slices about ⅜" (1 cm) from the edges and gently ease along the raffia. Tie lengths of raffia together as necessary to make the garland about 72" (183 cm) long. Form a loop at end; secure with knot.

HOW TO MAKE A WIRED-RIBBON GARLAND

MATERIALS

- Fabric.
- One or more rolls of paper-backed fusible web, ⅜" (1 cm) wide.
- 26-gauge beading wire or craft wire.

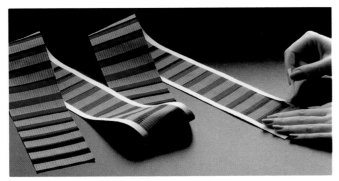

1 Cut fabric strips to desired width of ribbon plus ¾" (2 cm). Piece strips as necessary, as on page 50, step 7. Apply strip of fusible web to wrong side of fabric along both long edges, following the manufacturer's directions. Remove paper backing.

2 Cut wire slightly longer than the length of fabric. Place the wire along inner edge of one fused strip. Fold and press fused edge to wrong side of fabric, encasing wire. Repeat for opposite side. Trim wire at ends.

MORE IDEAS FOR GARLANDS

Spice garland is made by stringing spice ornaments (page 24) and cranberries to create a richly textured garland.

Metal garland is made by joining metal ornaments (page 29) with brass wire.

Dough-ornament garland with a country look consists of aromatic dough ornaments (page 26) strung on raffia. Make holes for stringing the ornaments before baking.

TREE TRIMMING

Collectible metal toys and cookie cutters *are used as ornaments to create a country-style tree. Popcorn garland and fabric bows are used for contrast, and raffia streamers add to the country look.*

A variety of ornaments can be mixed successfully on a tree. Create a unified look by emphasizing a particular color or style, repeating it in several areas of the tree. For interest, add a few elements of surprise, such as an artificial bird's nest, oversize decorations, dried or silk flowers, or raffia streamers.

Wired-ribbon bow *is used as a tree topper. Streamers of ribbon cascade down the tree and are tucked into the branches. Gold and bronze foliage and berry picks are tucked into the branches to complete the elegant look.*

Dried floral materials, *such as baby's breath, German statice, roses, and pepper berries, are tucked into the tree, creating a garland effect. Several craft bird's nests and birds add to the natural look. Dried flowers, tied with a bow, are used as a tree topper.*

Artificial fruit garland *gives a natural look to this tree. Aromatic dried-fruit-slice ornaments (pages 40 and 41) and honeysuckle vine are used to decorate the tree.*

Oversize decorations, *such as snowmen, can be used for impact on a tree. Place the oversize decorations on the tree first, securing them with floral wire, if necessary. Candy canes and frosted twigs are used to fill in bare areas.*

TREE SKIRTS

A tree skirt offers the finishing touch to a Christmas tree. This simple lined tree skirt, finished with bias binding, has a layer of polyester fleece or batting for added body. It can be embellished in a variety of ways, using fused appliqués.

Make the patterns for appliqué designs by enlarging simple motifs found on Christmas cards or gift-wrapping paper. Use machine quilting or hand stitching around the outer edges of the appliqués to give them more definition.

MATERIALS

- 1¼ yd. (1.15 m) fabric, for tree skirt.
- 1¼ yd. (1.15 m) lining fabric.
- 45" (115 cm) square polyester fleece or low-loft quilt batting.
- ¾ yd. (0.7 m) fabric, for binding.
- Scraps of fabric, for fused appliqués.
- Paper-backed fusible web.

CUTTING DIRECTIONS

Cut the fabric, lining, and fleece or batting as in steps 1 to 3, below. Cut bias fabric strips, 2½" (6.5 cm) wide, for the binding.

HOW TO SEW A TREE SKIRT

1 Fold fabric for tree skirt in half lengthwise, then crosswise. Using a straightedge and a pencil, mark an arc on the fabric, measuring 21" to 22" (53.5 to 56 cm) from folded center of fabric. Cut on the marked line through all layers.

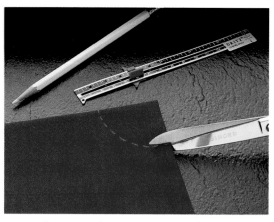

2 Mark a second arc, measuring 1¾" (4.5 cm) from the folded center of the fabric. Cut on the marked line.

3 Cut along one folded edge; this will be the center back. Cut lining and fleece or batting, using fabric for tree skirt as a pattern.

4 Apply the paper-backed fusible web to the wrong side of fabric scraps, following the manufacturer's directions. Transfer design motifs onto paper side of the fusible web; turn pattern over if the design is asymmetrical.

(Continued)

5 Cut design motifs from paper-backed fabric; remove paper backing. Fuse motifs to the tree skirt as desired.

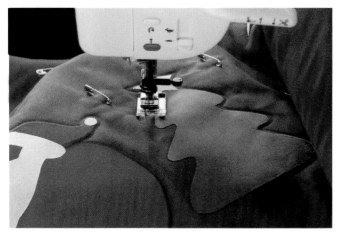

6 Layer the lining, fleece, and fabric for tree skirt, right sides out. Baste the layers together, using safety pins or hand stitching. Quilt design motifs by stitching around the outer edges of designs.

7 Piece binding strips to form 5½-yd. (5.05 m) length; join the strips together as shown; trim ¼" (6 mm) from stitching. Press seams open; trim off points.

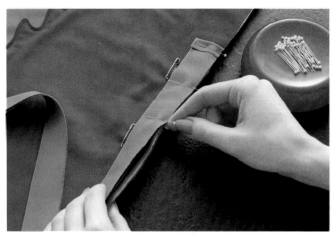

8 Press the binding strip in half lengthwise, wrong sides together; fold back ½" (1.3 cm) on one short end. Pin binding to tree skirt, matching raw edges and starting at center back.

9 Stitch a scant ⅜" (1 cm) from raw edges, overlapping ends of binding ½" (1.3 cm); trim close to stitching.

10 Wrap binding strip snugly around edge of tree skirt, covering the stitching line on the wrong side; pin. Stitch in the ditch on right side of tree skirt, catching the binding on the wrong side.

MORE IDEAS
FOR TREE
SKIRTS

Gingerbread-men appliqués
embellish this tree skirt. The outer
edge is defined with contrasting bias
binding and jumbo rickrack. The
rickrack is applied to the underside
of the tree skirt after the binding is
applied. The gingerbread men are
embellished with fabric paints in
fine-tip tubes.

Star-and-moon theme is created using appliqués from
lamé fabric. To prevent the delicate fabric from fraying,
the raw edges of the appliqués were sealed, using fabric
paints in fine-tip tubes.

Bullion fringe adds an elegant edging to a brocade tree
skirt. Applied to the underside of the tree skirt, the fringe
is secured in place by edgestitching along the inside edge
of the binding from the right side.

Sheer organza overlay,
placed over the fused
angel appliqués, creates a
shadow embroidery effect.
The tree skirt is quilted
around the outer edges of
the appliqués, using two
strands of embroidery
thread and a hand
running stitch.

The Holiday Table

FRESH FLORAL ARRANGEMENTS

Decorate for the holidays with fresh flowers by making a centerpiece or a buffet arrangement. A centerpiece used on a dining table is usually short in height so it does not interfere with conversation. A buffet arrangement is designed to be placed against a wall and can be taller, for more impact.

To make a holiday arrangement, use long-lasting flowers such as those on page 56 and add sprigs of greenery, such as Scotch pine, spruce, or juniper. For a more festive look, embellish the arrangement with canella berries, decorative pods, pepper berries, pinecones, feathers, or seeded eucalyptus.

A fresh holiday arrangement can be displayed in any container that holds water. For baskets, terra-cotta pots, or metal pots, use a plastic waterproof container as a liner.

Fresh flowers can be held in the arrangement by either of two methods, depending on the container selected. For glass containers, the flowers are held in place by making a grid over the mouth of the container with clear waterproof tape. For nonglass containers, the flowers are held in place by inserting them into floral foam designed for fresh flowers.

TIPS FOR FRESH FLOWERS

Cut off 1" (2.5 cm) from stems, at an angle, before arranging; for roses, cut stems at an angle while submerging them in water.

Remove any leaves that will be covered by water in the finished arrangement; leaves left in the water will shorten the life of the flowers.

Add cut-flower food to the water.

Add fresh water to the floral arrangement as necessary.

Keep flowers out of direct sunlight and drafts.

MATERIALS

- Flowers in three sizes.
- Sprigs of two or more varieties of greenery.
- Tall linear floral material, such as gilded devil's claw heliconia, curly willow, or branches, for the buffet arrangement.

- Gilded pods, berries, or twigs, for the centerpiece.
- Floral foam, designed for fresh flowers, for use with nonglass containers.
- Clear waterproof floral tape.
- Sharp knife.

Centerpiece (above) combines chrysanthemums, roses, ornithogalum, leatherleaf, seeded eucalyptus, lotus pods, and cedar. Buffet arrangement (opposite) uses mums, lilies, leptosporum, roses, gilded devil's claw heliconia, leatherleaf, and seeded eucalyptus to create a dramatic display.

Chrysanthemums

Ornithogalum

Lily

Carnations

Orchid

Yarrow

Heather

Roses

Alstroemeria

Stock

Leptosporum

Flowers shown above can be used to make long-lasting holiday arrangements.

HOW TO PREPARE THE CONTAINER

1 **Nonglass containers.** Soak the floral foam in water for at least 20 minutes.

2 Cut foam, using a knife, so it fits the container and extends about 1" (2.5 cm) above rim. Round off the upper edges of foam, if necessary, to prevent foam from showing in the finished arrangement. Secure with clear waterproof tape. Add water.

Glass containers. Make a grid over the mouth of container, using clear waterproof floral tape.

HOW TO MAKE A FRESH FLORAL BUFFET ARRANGEMENT

1 Prepare glass or nonglass container (above). Insert first variety of greenery into container, placing taller stems into center near back and shorter stems at sides and front.

2 Insert remaining varieties of greenery. Insert tall linear materials into container, spacing them evenly.

3 Insert largest flowers into the arrangement, one variety at a time, spacing them evenly throughout to keep arrangement balanced on three sides.

4 Insert second largest flowers into arrangement, spacing evenly. Insert the smaller flowers into the arrangement to fill any bare areas. Mist arrangement lightly with water.

HOW TO MAKE A FRESH FLORAL CENTERPIECE

1 Prepare the glass or nonglass container (opposite). Cut sprigs of greenery to lengths of 5" to 8" (12.5 to 20.5 cm); trim away any stems near the ends of sprigs.

2 Insert sprigs of greenery into the container, placing longer sprigs around the outside and shorter sprigs near the center.

3 Insert the largest flowers into the container, placing one stem in the center and several stems on each side to establish the height and width of the arrangement. Insert remaining large flowers, spacing evenly.

4 Insert the second largest flowers into the arrangement, one variety at a time, spacing evenly, so the arrangement appears balanced from all sides.

5 Insert additional sprigs of greenery as necessary to fill in any bare areas. Insert gilded pods, twigs, or berries, if desired, for further embellishment. Mist arrangement lightly with water.

Country arrangement *is created by filling small brown bags with popcorn, nuts, and dried fruits. The bags are tied with torn strips of fabric and placed in a rustic basket.*

Elegant decorating accent is created from a dried grapevine wreath, an artificial vine of grape leaves, dried artichokes, and gilded cones. Refer to pages 98 to 101 for information on embellishing wreaths.

Natural setting is created with a pine garland used as the base of the arrangement. Pillar candles placed in glasses and smaller votive candles are embellished with cinnamon sticks and raffia. Spice ornaments and dried flowers are scattered throughout, for additional interest.

HOLIDAY PLACEMATS & TABLE RUNNERS

Create a variety of looks for the holiday table using simple stitched-and-turned placemats and table runners. Choose to make placemats and a matching rectangular table runner, or sew a table runner that has pointed ends. Embellish the placemats and table runner with coordinating braid, ribbon, or other flat trims.

The instructions that follow are for placemats with a finished size of 13" × 18" (33 × 46 cm). The length of the table runner is determined by the length of the table and the desired drop length, or overhang, at the ends of the table.

MATERIALS (for four placemats)

- 1⅝ yd. (1.5 m) fabric, for the placemat top and backing pieces.
- 1⅝ yd. (1.5 m) fusible interfacing.
- Braid or other flat trim.

MATERIALS (for table runner)

- Fabric, for table runner top and backing pieces; yardage varies, depending on length of runner.
- Fusible or sew-in interfacing; yardage varies, depending on length of runner.
- Braid or other flat trim.

CUTTING DIRECTIONS

For each placemat, cut two 13½" × 18½" (34.3 × 47.3 cm) rectangles from fabric, for the placemat top and backing. Cut one 13½" × 18½" (34.3 × 47.3 cm) rectangle from fusible interfacing.

For a table runner, cut two rectangles from fabric for the table runner top and backing, and cut one rectangle from fusible interfacing. The width of the rectangles is 18½" (47.3 cm); the length is equal to the length of the table plus two times the desired drop length, plus ½" (1.3 cm) for the seam allowances.

HOW TO SEW A BASIC PLACEMAT OR TABLE RUNNER

1 Apply interfacing to the wrong side of placemat or table runner top; if using fusible interfacing, follow manufacturer's directions.

2 Pin top to backing, right sides together. Stitch around placemat or table runner, ¼" (6 mm) from raw edges; leave 4" (10 cm) opening for turning. Trim corners.

3 Turn the placemat or table runner right side out; press. Slipstitch the opening closed. If desired, embellish with braid trim (page 62).

HOW TO SEW A TABLE RUNNER WITH POINTED ENDS

1 Mark the center of one short end on rectangle for table runner top. From same short end, measure distance on each long edge equal to the desired drop length plus ¼" (6 mm) for seam allowance; mark. Draw lines from marking on short end to markings on long edges.

2 Fold rectangle for table runner top in half crosswise; align the raw edges. Cut on marked lines through both layers. Cut backing and interfacing to match table runner top. Complete table runner as on page 61, steps 1 to 3.

HOW TO EMBELLISH A PLACEMAT OR TABLE RUNNER
WITH BRAID TRIM

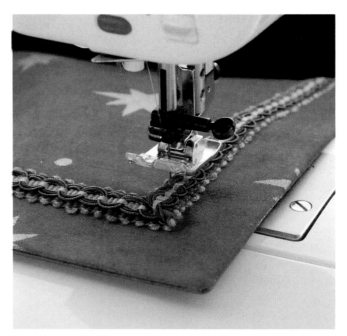

1 Pin braid trim to the placemat or table runner at desired distance from edge; miter the braid trim at corners by folding it at an angle. Fold end of braid diagonally at final corner; trim excess.

2 Edgestitch along inner and outer edges of braid trim; hand-stitch mitered corners in place.

MORE IDEAS FOR PLACEMATS & TABLE RUNNERS

Braid trim (left) is used to make a mitered border around a placemat.

Purchased appliqués add a festive touch to a plain placemat. The appliqués are fused to the placemat tops before the backing is applied.

Assorted trims (above) are stitched to the placemat top before the backing is applied.

Layered trims are positioned 1" (2.5 cm) from the outer edges of a pointed table runner (right). A tassel is stitched to each point.

PACKAGE PLACEMATS

Dress up a holiday table with pieced placemats that have the three-dimensional look of wrapped packages. The dimensional illusion is achieved by using fabrics in light, medium, and dark colors. A simple bow, created from a pleated fabric square and a fabric loop, completes the package.

The placemat is made from either lightweight cotton or cotton blends, using quick cutting and piecing techniques for easy construction. The instructions that follow are for a set of four placemats that measure about 13" × 17" (33 × 43 cm). Stitch the placemats using ¼" (6 mm) seam allowances.

MATERIALS (for four placemats)

- ¼ yd. (0.25 m) light-colored fabric, for package top.
- ½ yd. (0.5 m) medium-colored fabric, for package front.
- ¼ yd. (0.25 m) dark-colored fabric, for package side.
- ⅝ yd. (0.6 m) fabric, for ribbon and bow.
- ⅞ yd. (0.8 m) fabric, for backing.
- Low-loft quilt batting.
- Quilter's ruler with an edge at 45° angle.

CUTTING DIRECTIONS

Cut the following strips on the crosswise grain, cutting across the full width of the fabric: two 6½" (16.3 cm) strips from the fabric for the package front; two 2" (5 cm) strips from the fabric for the package side; and four 2" (5 cm) strips from the fabric for the package top. From the fabric for the ribbon and bow, cut: four 1½" (3.8 cm) strips and one 1¼" (3.2 cm) strip, for the ribbon; eight 6½" (16.3 cm) squares, for the bows; and one 2½" × 15" (6.5 × 38 cm) strip, for the loop of the bow. Cut four 13½" × 17½" (34.3 × 44.3 cm) rectangles each from the backing fabric and batting.

HOW TO SEW A SET OF PACKAGE PLACEMATS

1 Stitch package front strips to each side of one 1½" (3.8 cm) ribbon strip, to make pieced strip for package fronts. Press the seam allowances toward ribbon strip. From pieced strip, cut four 9½" × 13½" (24.3 × 34.3 cm) rectangles.

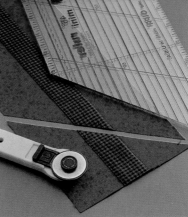

2 Stitch package side strips to each side of one 1½" (3.8 cm) ribbon strip, to make pieced strip for package sides. Press the seam allowances toward ribbon strip. Cut off one end of pieced strip at 45° angle, as shown.

(Continued)

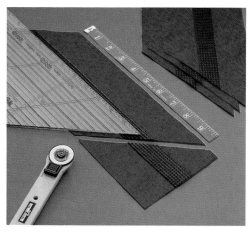

3 Measure and mark strip at 9¾" (25 cm) intervals. Cut four parallelograms for package sides, as shown.

4 Stitch package top strips to each side of one 1½" (3.8 cm) ribbon strip, to make the pieced strip for the package tops. Repeat to make two pieced strips. Press seam allowances toward ribbon strips. Cut off one end of each pieced strip at a 45° angle, as shown; the angle is cut in the opposite direction from the angle of package side strips.

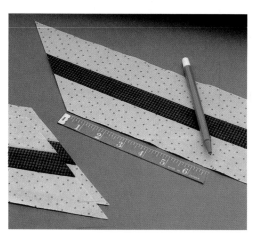

5 Measure and mark the package top strips at 6¾" (17 cm) intervals. Cut into eight parallelograms for package tops.

6 Stitch the 1¼" (3.2 cm) ribbon strip to one angled end of one of the parallelograms for package top; allow excess fabric from ribbon strip at each end. Press seam allowances toward ribbon strip; trim strip even with edges of the parallelogram. Stitch second parallelogram for package top to the opposite side of ribbon strip; press the seam allowances toward the ribbon strip. Repeat to make four package tops.

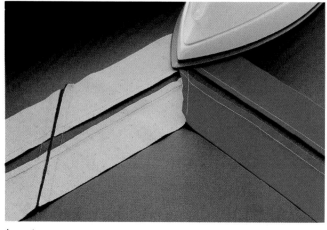

7 Align one package top to one package side along the angled edges, with right sides together and raw edges even. Stitch from sharply pointed end to ¼" (6 mm) from inside corner; backstitch to secure stitching. Press the seam allowances toward package top.

8 Align pieced strips for side and top to package front, matching ribbon strips of top and front. Stitch from outer edges exactly to the seam intersection. Press seam allowances toward top and side.

9 Place the backing and placemat top right sides together. Place fabrics on batting, with pieced design on top; pin or baste layers together.

10 Stitch around the placemat top, ¼" (6 mm) from raw edges; leave 4" (10 cm) opening for turning. Trim the excess backing and batting; trim corners.

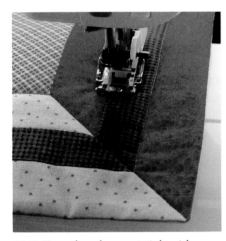

11 Turn the placemat right side out; press. Slipstitch opening closed. Quilt placemat by stitching on seamlines, using monofilament nylon thread in needle and thread that matches backing fabric in the bobbin. (Contrasting thread was used to show detail.)

12 Fold strip for loop of bow in half lengthwise, right sides together. Stitch ¼" (6 mm) seam; turn tube right side out. Press, with the seam centered on one side. Cut tube into four 3" (7.5 cm) strips.

13 Press raw edges ¼" (6 mm) to inside at one end of each tube; tuck opposite end inside the tube to make a loop. Stitch ends together. Pin loop, as shown, over intersecting ribbons on package top. Slipstitch in place.

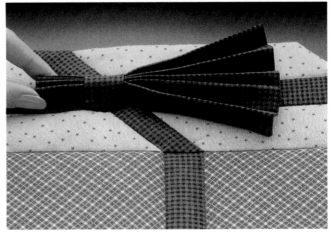

14 Place two fabric pieces for bow right sides together, matching raw edges. Stitch ¼" (6 mm) from raw edges, leaving 2" (5 cm) opening for turning. Trim the corners; press the seams open.

15 Turn bow piece right side out; press. Slipstitch the opening closed. Hand-pleat fabric, and insert into loop for bow.

PIECED STAR
TABLE TOPPERS

This eight-pointed reversible star adds a decorative touch to tables. Use it as a table topper over a skirted round table. Or drape it over a dining table, sofa table, or end table.

The star is made by stitching eight diamonds together. The outer half of each diamond is cut longer than the inner half, creating extended points that can be draped over the edges of a table. The finished star measures about 50" (127 cm) in diameter. Tassels can be added to the points of the stars for additional embellishment.

The star and the lining can be sewn from a single fabric. Or use two or more fabrics for variety. If more than one fabric is used, become familiar with the piecing technique in order to plan the placement of the pieces before you

begin to stitch. The lining is constructed using the same method as for the star, making the table topper reversible.

MATERIALS

- 3 yd. (2.75 m) fabric, for star and lining from one fabric, or ¾ yd. (0.7 m) each of four fabrics, for star and lining from four fabrics.
- Eight tassels, optional.

CUTTING DIRECTIONS

Make the pattern as on page 70. Cut eight diamonds from the fabric or fabrics for the star. Also cut eight diamonds from the fabric for the lining.

Pieced star table toppers can be made in a variety of styles. Above, the star topper with a country look is made from four different cotton fabrics. Opposite, an elegant star topper is made from a single fabric and embellished with tassels at each of the points.

HOW TO MAKE A PIECED STAR TABLE TOPPER PATTERN

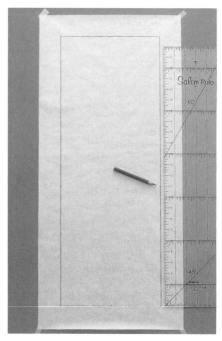

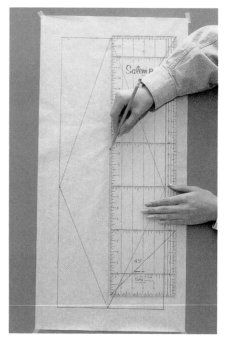

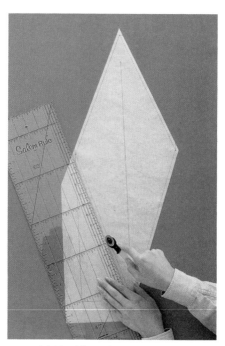

1 Draw 9¼" × 25" (23.6 × 63.5 cm) rectangle on paper. Mark a dot at the center of each short side. Mark a dot along each long side, 11" (28 cm) from one end.

2 Draw lines connecting the dots as shown. Mark grainline parallel to long sides of rectangle.

3 Add ¼" (6 mm) seam allowances to the diamond pattern, outside the marked lines. Cut out pattern.

HOW TO SEW A PIECED STAR TABLE TOPPER

1 Align two of the diamonds, right sides together and raw edges even. Stitch ¼" (6 mm) seam on one short side, stitching toward narrow point. Repeat for remaining pieces to make four 2-diamond units.

2 Stitch two of the 2-diamond units, right sides together, along one short side; finger-press seam allowances in opposite directions as shown. Repeat for the remaining two units.

3 Place the two 4-diamond units right sides together. Pin, matching inner points of diamonds at center. Fold seam allowances of each unit in opposite directions; stitch seam from outer edges toward center.

4 Release the stitching within the seam allowances at center of star, so seam allowances will lie flat. Press from wrong side, working from center out.

5 Repeat steps 1 to 4 for lining. Pin the star and the lining, right sides together, matching the raw edges and seams; the seam allowances will face in opposite directions. Stitch around star, stitching from inside corners to points; leave 6" (15 cm) opening on one side, for turning.

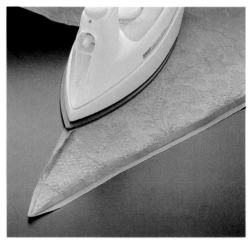

6 Clip inside corners, and trim points. Press the seam allowances open around the outer edges.

7 Turn star right side out; press. Slipstitch opening closed. Stitch a tassel to each point, if desired.

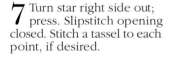

Around The House

JEWELED
TREE

Make an elegant jeweled tree to accent a holiday table or buffet. Or group several trees of various sizes together to create a mantel display. Simple to make, the jeweled tree is constructed by wrapping beaded garland and decorative cording around a Styrofoam® cone. The jeweled tree can be further embellished with miniature ornaments or topped with a folded star ornament (page 33).

To assemble the tree, the Styrofoam cone is mounted on a painted dowel and set in a container of plaster of Paris. To conceal the container, wrap it with a fabric circle, tied with decorative cording.

MATERIALS

- Styrofoam cone in desired size up to 15" (38 cm).
- Paper twist.
- One or two beaded garlands.
- Decorative cording.
- Wooden Shaker box, 4½" (11.5 cm) in diameter.
- Dowel, ⅝" (1.5 cm) in diameter.
- Aerosol acrylic paint in color that blends with colors of beaded garland and decorative cording, optional.
- ½ yd. (0.5 m) fabric, for base.
- ½ yd. (0.5 m) lining fabric, for base, if contrasting lining is desired.
- ½ yd. (0.5 m) decorative cording, for base.
- Plaster of Paris.
- Rubber band.
- Hot glue gun and glue sticks.
- Miniature ornaments or embellishments, optional.

CUTTING DIRECTIONS

Cut one 17" (43 cm) circle from the fabric and the lining, for the base. Cut a 1½" (3.8 cm) slit in the center of the lining circle.

HOW TO MAKE A JEWELED TREE

1 Line Shaker box with two layers of aluminum foil. Crumple the foil loosely to shape of the box, to allow room for the plaster to expand as it dries; edge of the foil should be ¼" (6 mm) below top of box.

2 Insert trunk of tree into cone to one-third the height of the cone. Place trunk in box, and adjust height of tree by cutting trunk to the desired length. Remove cone from trunk.

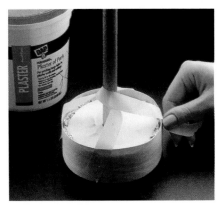

3 Mix the plaster of Paris, following manufacturer's directions. Pour plaster into box, filling to edge of foil. When the plaster has started to thicken, insert trunk, making sure it stands straight. Support the trunk as shown, until plaster has set.

4 Glue the paper twist around cone, piecing as necessary to cover the Styrofoam. Cut a circle of paper twist to the diameter of cone base; glue to bottom of cone. Spray the cone with aerosol acrylic paint, if desired.

5 Glue jeweled garland and cording alternately to cone in continuous rows, starting at lower edge; glue one row at a time. Continue until the cone is completely covered; add another garland, if necessary.

6 Apply hot glue into the hole in the Styrofoam cone and to the top of the trunk. Place cone on trunk.

7 Pin the circles right sides together; stitch ¼" (6 mm) from edge. Turn fabric circle right side out through the slit in lining; press.

8 Wrap the fabric circle around base of tree; secure around dowel with rubber band. Knot ends of cording; wrap the cording around the fabric circle, concealing the rubber band. Embellish tree with star or miniature decorations, if desired, securing them with hot glue.

FRINGED FABRIC TREE

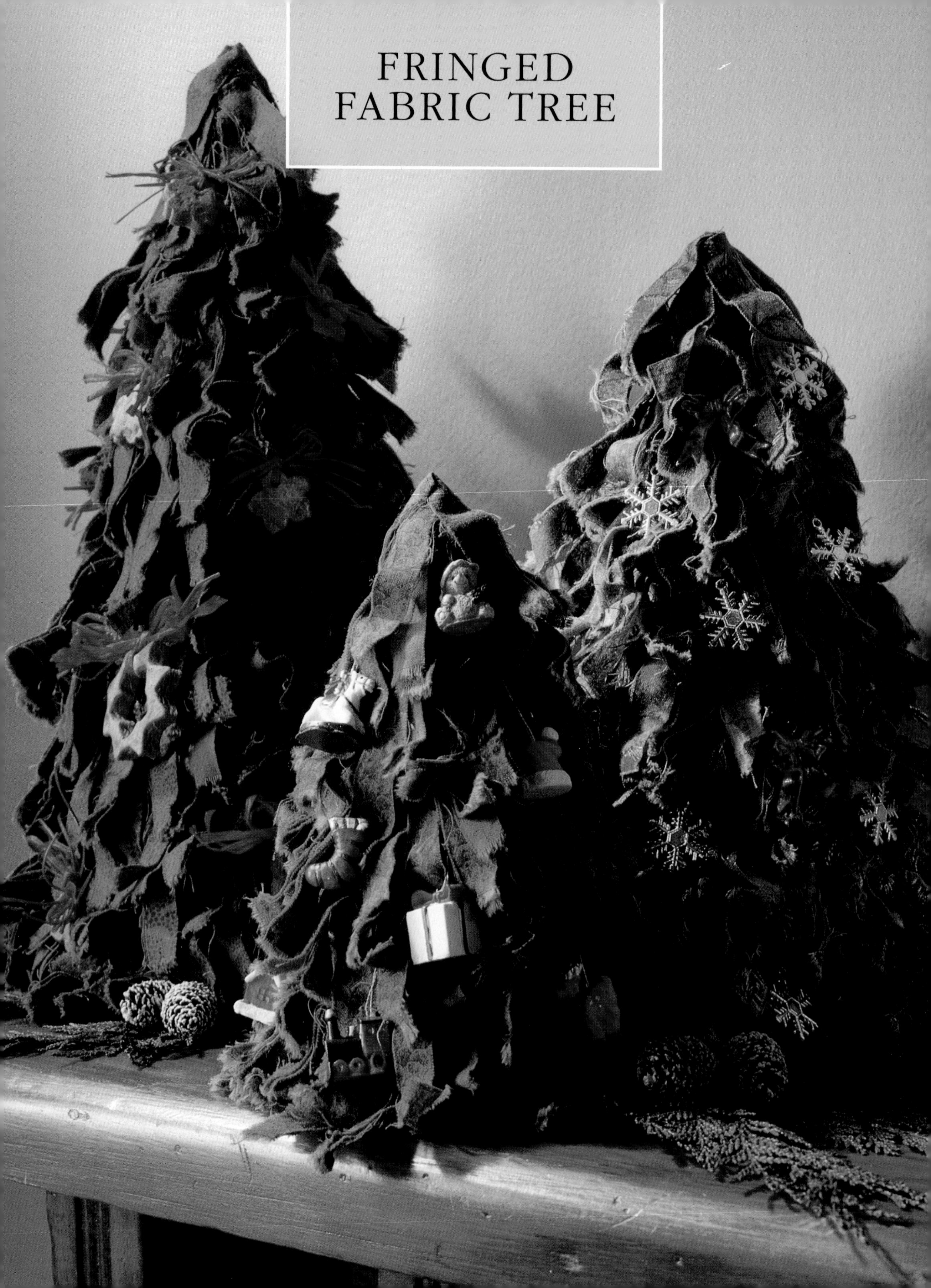

Make a grouping of fabric trees in various sizes to display on a mantel. The trees are made from fringed strips of cotton fabric that are wrapped around a Styrofoam® cone. The fringe is given a frayed appearance by wetting it, then machine drying it with towels. Decorate the trees with purchased decorations or miniature aromatic dough ornaments (page 26).

MATERIALS

- Styrofoam cone with height of 6" (15 cm), 9" (23 cm), or 12" (30.5 cm), depending on desired tree size.
- ½ yd. (0.5 m) fabric for small tree or ¾ yd. (0.7 m) for medium or large tree.
- Thick craft glue.
- 4" (10 cm) lengths of wire, for securing embellishments.
- Embellishments, such as miniature decorations and raffia, if desired.

HOW TO MAKE A FRINGED FABRIC TREE

1 Tear fabric strips, 4¼" (10.8 cm) wide, on crosswise grain; reserve sufficient fabric for covering cone. Fold fabric strip in half lengthwise, wrong sides together; edgestitch close to fold. Repeat for remaining strips.

2 Make the fringe by clipping the strips at ½" (1.3 cm) intervals, along the edges opposite the fold; clip to, but not through, stitching. Wet clipped strips, and squeeze out any excess water; machine dry with towels to create frayed edges.

3 Trim Styrofoam cone to a point. Roll trimmed end gently on table to make smooth.

4 Wrap fabric around the Styrofoam cone; trim off excess. Secure fabric to cone, using craft glue.

5 Apply glue to upper edge of the fringe, gluing about 4" (10 cm) at a time. Wrap fringe around the cone, starting 1" (2.5 cm) from lower edge of tree; continue to glue and wrap fringe to end of strip.

6 Continue to glue and wrap additional fringed fabric strips around cone until entire cone is covered; overlap ends of strips slightly. Trim off excess at top.

7 Embellish tree as desired, securing ornaments to tree with bent lengths of wire.

FATHER CHRISTMAS

Decorate for the holidays with a handcrafted Father Christmas. The ones shown here have a simple stitched-and-turned body made from wool and are trimmed with scraps of fur. The face and mittens are shaped from polymer clay, using simple clay-modeling techniques; then they are baked and painted. A Father Christmas can be traditional or country in style, depending on the fabrics and accessories used.

MATERIALS

- ½ yd. (0.5 m) fabric, for body.
- Scraps of fur or fake fur, for trimming garment.
- Lightweight and heavyweight cardboard, for base.
- Polyester fiberfill.
- Natural or white unspun wool.
- Polymer clay, such as Sculpey® or Fimo®, in a light color.
- Rolling pin; paring knife.
- Acrylic paints, for face and mittens; artist's brushes.
- Glossy wood-tone floral spray, optional.
- Thick craft glue; hot glue gun and glue sticks.
- Accessories, such as miniature wreath, tree, presents, or stocking.

CUTTING DIRECTIONS

Trace the partial pattern pieces (page 123). Make full-size patterns for the body and the base, and cut the pieces as on page 80, steps 1 to 3.

Country-style Father Christmas *(above), made from plaid wool, holds a miniature artificial pine tree and grapevine wreath. The traditional fur-trimmed Father Christmas (opposite) carries a bag filled with miniature gifts and a small artificial pine wreath.*

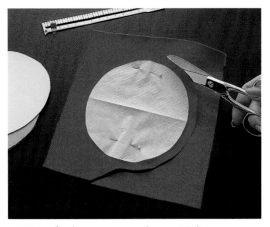

1 Transfer base pattern (page 123) to paper; fold the paper on dotted line, and cut on marked line. Using the pattern, cut one base piece from lightweight cardboard and another from heavyweight cardboard. Cut one fabric piece, adding ⅜" (1 cm) seam allowance.

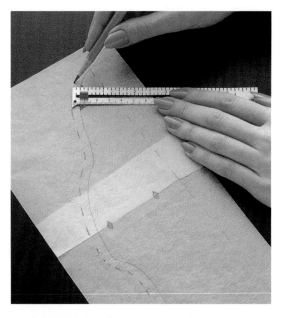

2 Transfer body pattern pieces A and B (page 123) to paper; tape them together, matching the notches and dotted lines. Add ¼" (6 mm) seam allowances around the sides and add ⅜" (1 cm) seam allowance along lower edge.

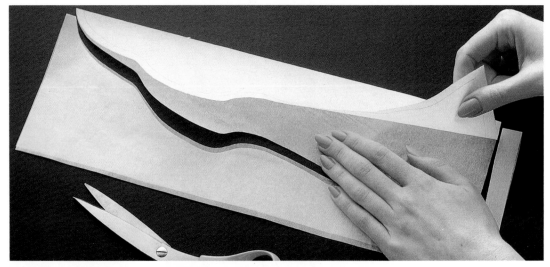

3 Transfer pattern from step 2 onto paper; fold on the dotted line. Cut on the outer lines and open the full-size pattern. Cut two body pieces from the fabric.

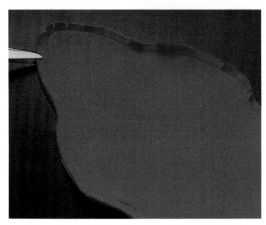

4 Pin pieces right sides together. Stitch ¼" (6 mm) seam around the sides, using short stitch length; leave the lower edge open. Clip the curves.

5 Turn body right side out. Stuff body firmly with polyester fiberfill to ⅜" (1 cm) from lower edge; use handle of wooden spoon to pack the fiberfill tightly.

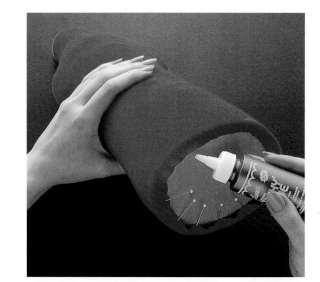

6 Insert the heavyweight cardboard base into body. Fold lower ⅜" (1 cm) of fabric over the cardboard; pin in place. Secure to cardboard, using craft glue.

7 Center lightweight cardboard base over the wrong side of fabric base. Wrap and glue edges of fabric around the cardboard, clipping fabric as necessary.

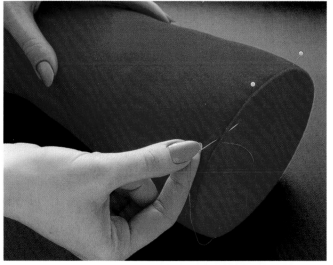

8 Place fabric-covered base over bottom of body, fabric side facing out; pin. Slipstitch in place.

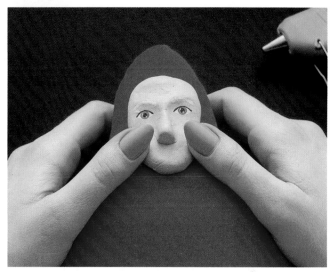

9 Make polymer clay face and mittens as on pages 82 and 83. Secure face to body, using hot glue.

10 Arrange unspun wool around face to create hair, beard, and moustache; secure with hot glue.

11 Cut ¾" (2 cm) fur strips for trim on the hat, garment center front, and lower edge as desired. Position the strips on Father Christmas; secure with hot glue.

(Continued)

12 Position mittens on body, adding any embellishments that will be held in hands; secure with hot glue.

13 Cut fur strips for cuffs, measuring about ¾" × 1½" (2 × 3.8 cm). Position over mittens at the wrist area; secure with hot glue. Attach additional embellishments.

HOW TO MAKE A FACE & MITTENS FROM POLYMER CLAY

1 Trace the pattern for mitten (page 123) onto tracing paper; cut on the marked line. Roll polymer clay to a thickness of about ³⁄₁₆" (4.5 mm), using a brayer or rolling pin. Place pattern on clay; cut out one mitten, using paring knife. Turn the pattern over; cut out other mitten. Smooth the edges of mittens, using fingers.

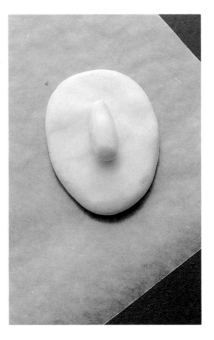

2 Shape an oval from the clay, measuring about 1½" × 2" (3.8 × 5 cm), for face. Roll a small piece of clay to form a rod, about ¼" (6 mm) in diameter; trim to ¾" (2 cm) in length. Center clay rod vertically on the face about ⅝" (1.5 cm) below one narrow edge of oval.

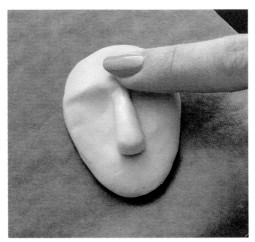

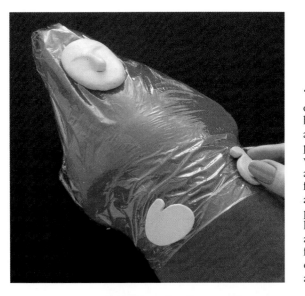

3 Smooth the edges of rod with fingers, blending clay into face to form nose. Shape brow, using fingers.

4 Place sheet of plastic wrap over assembled body. Position face and mittens over plastic and body, with top of face about 1" (2.5 cm) from top of body and the mittens positioned to hold any desired accessories. Shape face and mittens to curve of body or accessories.

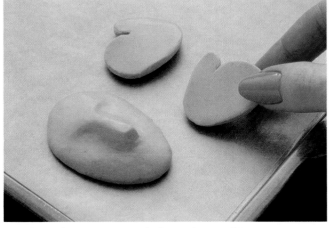

5 Place clay pieces on a baking sheet, taking care not to distort curved shape; bake in 225°F (107°C) preheated oven for 25 minutes. Allow clay to cool.

6 Paint mittens, using acrylic paint. Paint face in desired skin tone; when dry, apply small amount of blush-tone paint to cheeks, blending the color. Using a pencil, mark placement for eyes, spacing them as indicated in step 7.

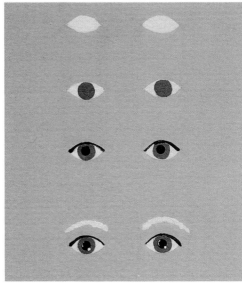

7 Paint the eyes and eyebrows as shown. (Photo shows actual size and spacing.)

8 Apply glossy wood-tone floral spray, if desired, to soften paint lines and give an old-fashioned quality to the face.

Pose an elf or two on a table or mantel to add a whimsical touch to your holiday decorating. The body of the elf is stuffed with polyester fiberfill and is weighted down with a small bag of sand. Small quantities of sand are available, packaged as paint additives, at many paint stores.

MATERIALS

- Fabric scraps.
- 3" (7.5 cm) square of paper-backed fusible web.
- Assorted two-hole or four-hole buttons.
- Two small shank buttons, for eyes.
- Polyester fiberfill.
- Sand; plastic bag, such as a sandwich bag.
- Jute and ¼" (6 mm) dowel, for hair.
- Hot glue gun and glue sticks.
- Heavy-duty thread, such as carpet thread.
- Pink cosmetic blush.
- Embellishments as desired.

CUTTING DIRECTIONS

Make the full-size patterns for the upper body, lower body, and hat as in steps 1 to 3, opposite. Cut two lower body pieces and two upper body pieces from scraps of fabric for the body. Using the pattern for the upper body, also cut two hat pieces from scraps of fabric for the hat.

Trace the pattern pieces for the boot and ear (page 123) onto paper. Cut four boots and four ears from scraps of fabric.

For the pants legs, cut two 5½" × 6" (14 × 15 cm) rectangles from scraps of fabric that match the lower body. For the sleeves, cut two 4½" × 5½" (11.5 × 14 cm) rectangles from scraps of fabric that match the upper body.

1 Draw a 9½" (24.3 cm) vertical line on center of tracing paper. Draw a perpendicular line at lower end, 3¼" (8.2 cm) long. Mark a point 3½" (9 cm) above lower edge and 2½" (6.5 cm) from vertical line. Mark a second point 6½" (16.3 cm) above lower edge and 1¾" (4.5 cm) from vertical line.

2 Connect points to perpendicular lines, curving the line slightly. Fold on vertical line; cut on the marked lines. Unfold paper.

3 Draw line 3½" (9 cm) above lower edge, perpendicular to vertical line. Cut off lower portion on marked line; this section is pattern for lower body of elf. Remaining section is pattern for upper body and also for hat. Transfer the patterns to paper, adding ¼" (6 mm) seam allowances.

4 Cut body pieces from fabric (opposite). Apply paper-backed fusible web to scrap of fabric for face, following manufacturer's directions. Cut an oval for face, about 2" (5 cm) long and 2¼" (6 cm) wide, from paper-backed fabric.

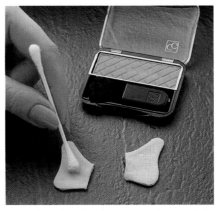

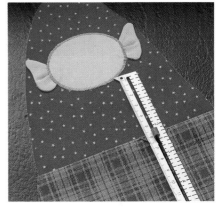

5 Align upper and lower front body sections, right sides together; stitch ¼" (6 mm) seam. Repeat for the back body sections, leaving a 3" (7.5 cm) opening in center of seam.

6 Stitch ⅛" (3 mm) seam around the ears, using short stitch length; leave straight edges open. Turn ears right side out, and press. Using cotton swab, rub pink blush in center of ears.

7 Remove paper backing from face. Make ⅛" (3 mm) tuck along the straight edge of each ear; baste to wrong side of face. Center face on upper body, with the face about 2¼" (6 cm) above the body seam. Fuse in place. Stitch around the face, using a narrow zigzag stitch.

(Continued)

8 Fold rectangle for sleeve in half, right sides together, matching short edges; stitch ¼" (6 mm) seam. Press seam open; turn tube right side out. Center the seam down front of tube. Make four ⅛" (3 mm) tucks, spaced evenly along upper edge of tube, so width is about 1½" (3.8 cm).

9 Pin tucked end of sleeve, seam side down, to right side of front upper body; match raw edges, and position sleeve about 1" (2.5 cm) above body seam. Baste. Repeat for other sleeve.

10 Fold rectangle for pants leg, right sides together, matching short edges; stitch ¼" (6 mm) seam. Press seam open; turn tube right side out. Center seam down back of tube. Repeat for other pants leg. Pin upper edge of pants legs to lower edge of front body section, centering them and matching raw edges; baste.

11 Pin front and back body sections right sides together. Stitch ¼" (6 mm) seam around body, taking care not to catch sleeves, pants legs, and ears in stitching.

12 Push in lower corners of elf, from right side, to shape the box corners. Slipstitch, or turn inside out and machine-stitch, across corners; turn right side out.

13 Roll up sleeves and pants legs. Thread needle with heavy-duty thread; secure thread to body, centered inside one pants leg. Thread a 2¾" (7 cm) strand of buttons, then thread back through the opposite holes of buttons; adjust the strand so top button of strand dangles about 3" (7.5 cm) below body. Secure thread. Repeat for other leg.

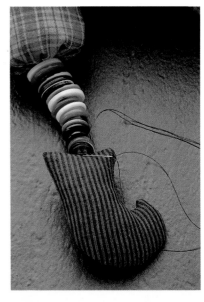

14 Stuff pants legs lightly with polyester fiberfill. On each pants leg, fold lower ¼" (6 mm) to the inside. Using hand running stitches, stitch close to the fold and tightly gather pants legs above buttons; secure thread.

15 Stitch ⅛" (3 mm) seam around the boot, using short stitch length; leave upper edge open. Clip inner curve. Turn right side out; stuff with polyester fiberfill. On each boot, fold upper ¼" (6 mm) to inside; slipstitch closed. Stitch the center of each boot to lower button of each button strand for legs.

16 Secure heavy-duty thread to body, centered inside one sleeve. Thread a 3" (7.5 cm) strand of buttons; secure thread inside other sleeve, allowing button strand to dangle from body about 2" (5 cm) at each side. Stuff sleeves and gather above buttons as in step 14.

17 Place about ⅔ cup (150 mL) sand in plastic bag. Tape bag closed, allowing space inside for sand to shift easily; this makes it easier for elf to sit. Insert the bag into the lower portion of body. Stuff remainder of body with polyester fiberfill; slipstitch opening closed.

18 Sew on buttons for the eyes; insert needle from back of body, and pull thread taut for a slight indentation. Rub pink blush on the face, for cheeks. Make jute hair, if desired, as on page 18, step 15; remove jute from dowel. Cut lengths of jute, and glue around face for the hair and beard.

19 Pin the hat pieces right sides together; stitch ¼" (6 mm) seam around curved sides. Turn right side out. Sew on buttons as desired at top of hat. Fold lower ¼" (6 mm) of hat to inside. Using hand running stitches, stitch close to fold; gather hat to fit head. Glue the hat to the elf. Secure any additional embellishments.

WOODEN CUTOUTS

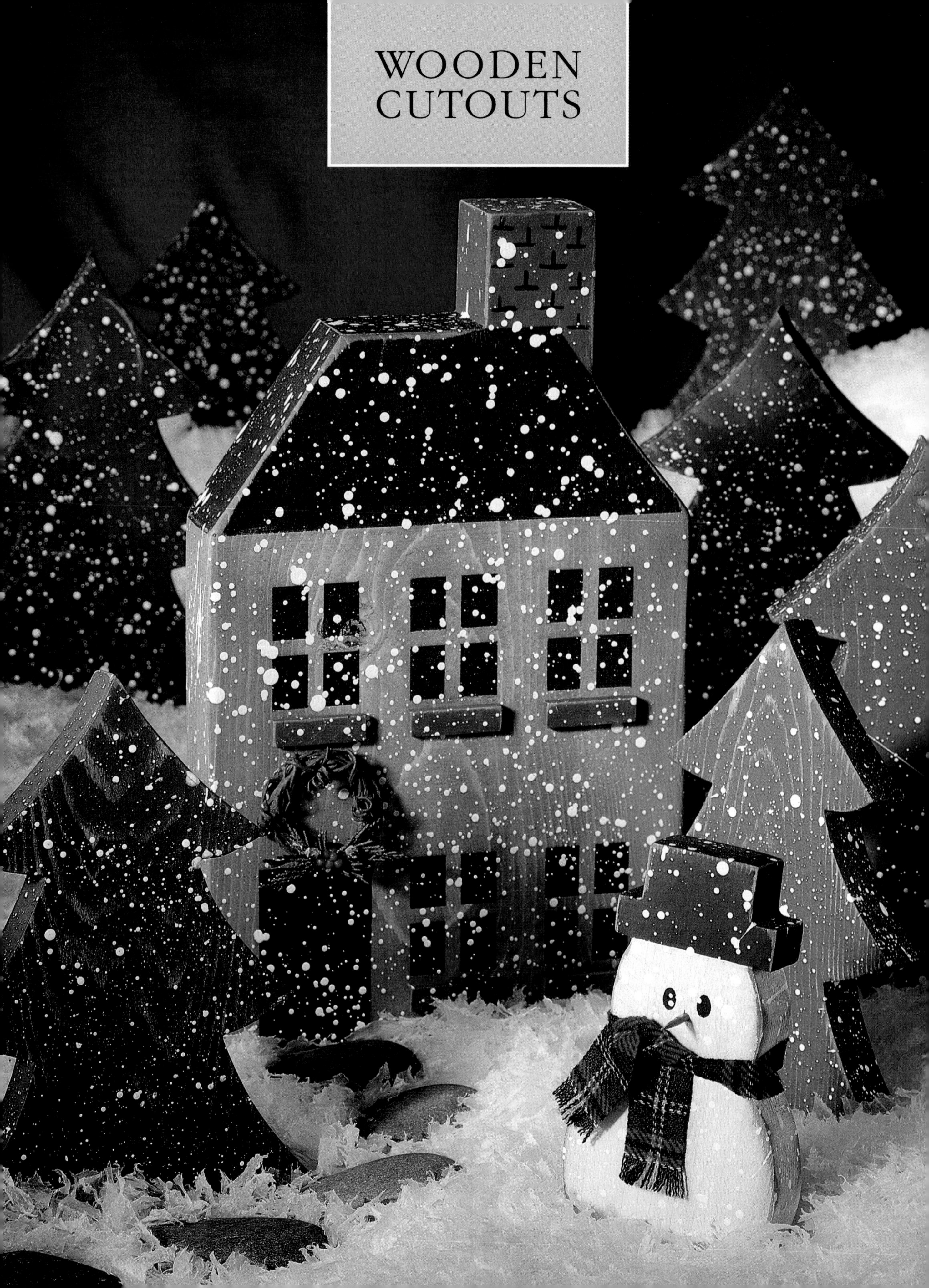

Create a winter scene with a wooden cutout village. This village is easily made using basic carpentry skills. Distressed edges and antiquing emphasize the handcrafted quality of the pieces.

The village pieces are made from scraps of pine lumber. Pine is easily cut with a jigsaw, and any imperfections in cutting can be sanded smooth. It is not necessary for the pieces to be cut symmetrically. Subtle variations add to the style. When cutting with a jigsaw, clamp the wood in place, protecting it, if necessary, by placing scrap blocks of wood or small felt pads between the workpiece and the clamp. Hold the saw tightly against the workpiece to reduce vibration, and move the saw smoothly while cutting. Cut curves with a fine-toothed scroll-cut blade, and use a slower speed to avoid bending the blade.

To give the cutouts an old-fashioned country look, paint them with acrylic paints in muted colors. Use off-white paint for the snowman and spattered snow.

MATERIALS

- Scraps of pine lumber: 2 × 8 pine lumber for house and large tree; 1 × 6 for small tree; 1 × 4 for snowman.
- Jigsaw; drill and 3/32" drill bit.
- Sanding block; medium-grit and fine-grit sandpaper.
- Acrylic paints; artist's brushes.
- 1" or 1½" (2.5 or 3.8 cm) synthetic-bristle paintbrush, for spattering.
- Transfer paper; masking tape, mat knife; wood glue or thick craft glue; hot glue gun and glue sticks.
- Stain in medium color, such as medium walnut.
- Embellishments for house, such as a miniature wreath or garland.
- Round toothpick and scrap of fabric, for snowman.
- Balsa wood molding strip in 1/8" (3 mm) thickness and desired width, for flower boxes.

HOW TO MAKE A WOODEN CUTOUT HOUSE

1 Cut a sheet of paper to width of 2 × 8 board and about 12" (30.5 cm) high. Draw roofline and chimney, using guide on page 124. Transfer guideline to wood, using transfer paper.

2 Cut along the marked lines, using jigsaw. Sand the wood smooth, using medium-grit sandpaper. Fold the sandpaper in thirds to sand the corners, curves, and edges.

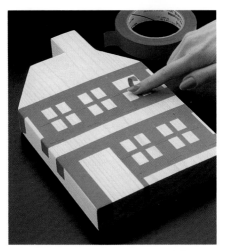

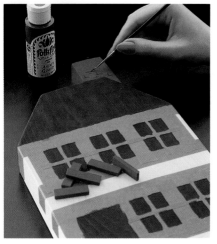

3 Mark doors and windows on front of house as desired, using masking tape. Mark mullions, using 1/4" (6 mm) strips of masking tape.

4 Mark the roofline with masking tape. Cut window boxes to size from balsa wood, using mat knife.

5 Paint the doors, windows, roof, and window boxes as desired. Allow to dry; remove tape. Paint chimney; add random strokes to represent bricks.

(Continued)

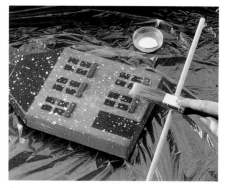

6 Sand edges of house and window boxes lightly, using a fine-grit sandpaper, to remove some paint and give an aged look. Apply stain to all pieces, using soft cloth; allow to dry. Secure window boxes with wood glue or thick craft glue.

7 Thin paint for snow, mixing two parts paint with one part water. Protect work surface with drop cloths or newspapers. Dip tip of brush into paint. Hold stick and paintbrush over project; strike brush handle against stick to spatter paint.

8 Place wreath over door; secure with hot glue. Attach additional embellishments as desired.

HOW TO MAKE A WOODEN CUTOUT SNOWMAN

1 Trace pattern (page 124) onto paper. Transfer pattern to wood, using transfer paper.

2 Cut along the marked lines, using a jigsaw. Starting at edge of board, cut along the upper half of top curve. Then, starting at edge of board, cut along lower edge of hat; this will remove wedge of wood. Continue cutting out remainder of snowman.

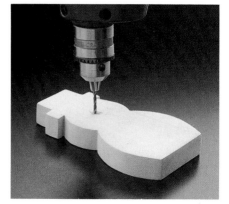

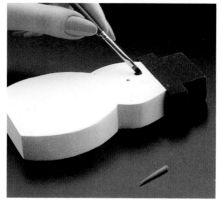

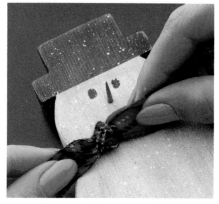

3 Sand the snowman as on page 89, step 2. Using a ³⁄₃₂" drill bit, drill hole about ³⁄₈" (1 cm) deep, for nose.

4 Paint the snowman, using artist's brush. Break off ⁷⁄₈" (2.2 cm) length of toothpick; paint orange. Transfer markings for eyes, if desired, using transfer paper. Paint eyes.

5 Follow step 6 above; insert the toothpick nose into the hole, gluing in place. Continue as in step 7, above. Cut ¾" × 12" (2 × 30.5 cm) fabric strip; tie around neck, for scarf.

HOW TO MAKE A WOODEN CUTOUT TREE

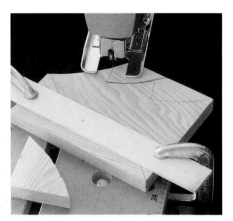

1 Trace desired tree pattern (page 124) onto paper; fold paper on the dotted line. Cut on the marked line to make full-size pattern. Transfer the pattern to wood, using transfer paper.

2 Cut along marked lines, using a jigsaw; cut curves from the edge of board to inside corners.

3 Sand the tree as on page 89, step 2. Paint the tree, using artist's brush, allowing the grain of wood to show through in some areas. Complete the tree as in steps 6 and 7, opposite.

MORE IDEAS FOR WOODEN CUTOUTS

Gingerbread house is decorated with purchased wooden cutouts and painted candy canes.

Personalized house is painted to resemble the owner's home. Snow paste adds texture to the roof.

Wooden blocks, cut from a 2 × 4 board, are painted with simple lettering and Christmas motifs for a holiday display.

BIAS-TRIMMED STOCKINGS

Large stockings, waiting to be filled with candy and trinkets, set the mood for the holiday season. A bias-trimmed stocking can be made in a variety of styles, depending on the choice of fabric and types of embellishments used. For a simple stocking, choose fabric that is distinctive and add embellishments such as purchased appliqués, ribbons, and buttons.

Make the binding from matching or contrasting fabric; a striped or plaid fabric can be used to create interesting effects. The stocking is lined and has a layer of fleece for added body.

MATERIALS

- ¾ yd. (0.7 m) outer fabric.
- ¾ yd. (0.7 m) lining fabric.
- ½ yd. (0.5 m) fabric, for bias binding.
- Polyester fleece.
- Embellishments, such as purchased appliqués, ribbon, or buttons.

CUTTING DIRECTIONS

Make the stocking pattern (below). With the right sides of the fabric together, cut two stocking pieces from the outer fabric and two from the lining. Also cut two stocking pieces from polyester fleece. Cut bias fabric strips, 2½" (6.5 cm) wide, for the binding, cutting two 10" (25.5 cm) strips for the upper edges of the stocking and one 60" (152.5 cm) strip for the sides. Piece the strips as necessary, as on page 50, step 7.

HOW TO MAKE A STOCKING PATTERN

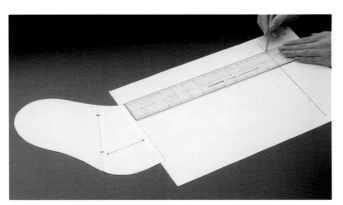

1 Transfer partial pattern pieces A and B (page 125) to paper. Tape pieces together, matching notches. Tape a large piece of paper to upper edge of partial stocking. Draw a line parallel to and 13" (33 cm) above dotted line, to mark upper edge of stocking. Align quilter's ruler to dotted line at side; mark point on line for upper edge. Repeat for the other side.

2 Measure out ⅞" (2.2 cm) from the marked points; mark. Connect the outer points at the upper edge to sides at ends of dotted line, to make full-size stocking pattern.

HOW TO SEW A BIAS-TRIMMED STOCKING

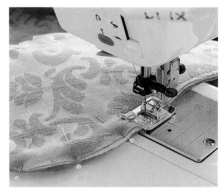

1 Layer the stocking front, fleece, and lining, right sides out. Baste layers together a scant ¼" (6 mm) from raw edges. Repeat for stocking back.

2 Position flat embellishments on the stocking as desired; pin or glue-baste in place. Stitch close to edges of trims.

3 Press the binding strips in half lengthwise, wrong sides together. Pin one 10" (25.5 cm) binding strip to upper edge of stocking front, right sides together, matching raw edges; stitch scant ⅜" (1 cm) seam.

4 Wrap binding around upper edge, covering stitching line on back of stocking; pin. Stitch in the ditch on the right side of stocking, catching binding on stocking back. Trim ends of binding even with stocking. Apply binding to upper edge of stocking back.

5 Align stocking front and back, with lining sides together; pin. Pin the binding to the stocking front, matching raw edges, with right sides together and ends extending ¾" (2 cm) on toe side of the stocking and 6" (15 cm) on the heel side; excess binding on the heel side becomes the hanger. Stitch scant ⅜" (1 cm) from raw edges; ease binding at heel and toe.

6 Fold the short end of the binding over upper edge of stocking. Wrap the binding around edge of stocking, covering stitching line on back; pin.

7 Fold up ½" (1.3 cm) on the end of the extended binding. Press up ¼" (6 mm) on raw edges of the extended binding. Fold the binding in half lengthwise, encasing the raw edges; pin. Edgestitch along pinned edges of the binding, for hanger. Stitch in the ditch around remainder of binding as in step 4.

8 Fold the extended binding strip to the back of stocking, forming a loop for hanger. Hand-stitch in place.

9 Hand-stitch ribbons, bows, or other embellishments to stocking front, if desired.

MORE IDEAS FOR BIAS-TRIMMED STOCKINGS

Written verses from "Jingle Bells" cover the front of this stocking. The verses are written using fine-point permanent-ink markers.

Buttons, stitched to the top of the stocking, give the appearance of a cuff.

Tea-dyed fabrics give a homespun look to this stocking. Fused appliqués are applied to the stocking front, using paper-backed fusible web as on pages 48 and 50. Fabric paint is used to personalize the stocking.

DECORATING MANTELS

Family photographs *from previous Christmases are grouped on a mantel for a nostalgic look. Honeysuckle vine and dried hydrangeas are used to embellish the artificial garland.*

Mantels are the perfect place to showcase Christmas decorations. Evergreen boughs or garlands displayed on a mantel can serve as a backdrop for a collection of family photos, Santas, unique ornaments, or hand-crafted Christmas items. For interest, mix a few dried or artificial floral elements with traditional Christmas accessories.

Safety note: *Do not leave any open flame, including candles, unattended.*

Gilded reindeer
and candles in brass
candlesticks (above)
are arranged on an
ornate mantel with
greenery, cones,
and berries. The
papier-mâché
reindeer were gilded
with metallic paint.

Amaryllis (right)
are set on each
side of a picture,
dominating this
Christmas display.

Countdown calendar (below) is made by hanging twenty-four tea-dyed stocking ornaments (page 21), filled with
holiday candies, along a fresh garland. A star ornament hangs at the end of the garland for Christmas Day.

EMBELLISHING
WREATHS

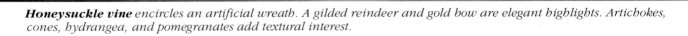

Honeysuckle vine *encircles an artificial wreath. A gilded reindeer and gold bow are elegant highlights. Artichokes, cones, hydrangea, and pomegranates add textural interest.*

Wreaths can be embellished for a variety of looks. For the base, select a fresh or artificial evergreen wreath, or a grapevine wreath. Embellish the base with items such as ribbons, ornaments, and floral materials to create a wreath that reflects your personal style.

Artificial evergreen wreaths are especially easy to decorate, because many items can be secured by simply twisting the branches around the embellishments. Items can also be secured to wreaths using floral wire or hot glue.

Embellish wreaths with one material at a time, spacing the items evenly to achieve a balanced look. Add large items first and fill in any bare areas with smaller ones. Secure embellishments to the surface as well as to the wreath base, to give a sense of depth.

Artificial evergreen garland *is wrapped around a grapevine wreath. A natural look is created by adding birch bark and twig birdhouses, artificial birds, and stems of rose hips.*

Santa's elf *(page 84) is wired to the center area of this fresh wreath to create a focal point. Dried fruit slices, cinnamon sticks, and paper twist are added to give this wreath a country look.*

Wire-mesh bow *(page 15) and metal ornaments (page 29) are used to embellish a fresh evergreen wreath. The mesh strips for the bow measure about 4" (10 cm) wide and 24" (61 cm) long. Lights were added to the wreath before it was decorated.*

Village house *becomes the focal point of an artificial wreath. Additional sprigs of greenery, cones, and berries are added for texture and fullness. For a snowy effect, aerosol artificial snow is sprayed over polyester fiberfill.*

TIPS FOR EMBELLISHING WREATHS

Attach wire to a cone by wrapping the wire around bottom layers of cone. Attach wire to a cinnamon stick by inserting it through length of stick; wrap wire around stick, and twist the ends at the middle.

Make floral or berry clusters by grouping items together. Attach wire to the items as necessary. Wrap stems and wires with floral tape.

Add texture to a wreath by inserting sprigs of other evergreen varieties. Secure sprigs to the wreath base, using wire.

Display Christmas collectibles, such as village houses and ornaments, on a wreath for visual impact. Wire items securely to the wreath base.

Gild embellishments, such as twigs, cones, artichokes, and sprigs of greenery, by applying gold aerosol acrylic paint.

Embellish wreath with ribbon by weaving it through the wreath; create twists and turns for depth. Secure the ribbon as necessary with hot glue.

Wrap honeysuckle vine loosely over a wreath, for added texture. Secure the vine with floral wire or hot glue.

Wrap artificial garland around a grapevine wreath to add color and dimension.

Add battery-operated lights to a wreath by weaving the cords into the wreath boughs.

Embellish bows with additional loops of contrasting ribbon. Fold length of ribbon in half to form loop the same size as loops on the existing bow; wrap ends tightly with wire. Secure to the center of bow, using hot glue.

GRAHAM CRACKER VILLAGE

Delight your family and guests with these charming variations on the traditional gingerbread house. Make one building or create a whole village. The graham cracker cottage, general store, and church can be embellished in a variety of ways with small candies, cookies, and cake decorations. To create a scene, accessorize the village with gumdrop shrubs, sugar-cone trees, and village people.

The buildings are constructed from graham cracker bricks that are held together with mortar made from melted white candy coating. To make the bricks, cut the graham crackers along the perforations. The patterns for the village buildings call for whole bricks, three-quarter bricks, half bricks, and one-quarter bricks. The candy coating used for mortar can be melted either on the stove or in a microwave oven.

COOKING DIRECTIONS FOR THE MORTAR

For the stovetop method, melt the candy coating in a small saucepan over low heat, stirring constantly. Thin the coating, if necessary, by adding ¼ teaspoon (1 mL) of vegetable shortening per ⅛ lb. (60 g) of candy coating.

For the microwave method, place ⅛ lb. (60 g) of the candy coating (one square) in a small bowl and microwave at 50% (Medium) for 2 to 3 minutes. Melt only one square at a time, because the coating hardens quickly as it cools.

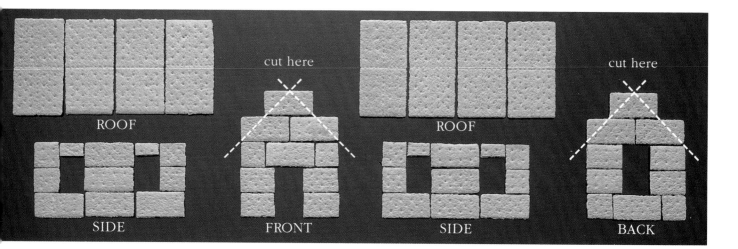

GRAHAM CRACKER COTTAGE

MATERIALS

- Twenty-eight whole graham crackers.
- 1½ lbs. (750 g) white candy coating.
- Multicolored hard candies.
- Multicolored fruit-flavored gumdrop slices.
- Red licorice.

- Red shoestring licorice.
- Red cinnamon candies.
- Round peppermint candies.
- Silver balls.
- Cream-filled wafer cookies, 2½" (6.5 cm) long.
- Multicolored candy-coated licorice pieces.

- Multicolored shot.
- 1-qt. (1 L) sealable freezer bags.
- Sturdy cardboard.
- Wax paper.
- Baking sheet.
- 8" (20.5 cm) chef's knife.

PATTERNS FOR A GRAHAM CRACKER COTTAGE

ROOF   cut here

ROOF   cut here

SIDE   FRONT   SIDE   BACK

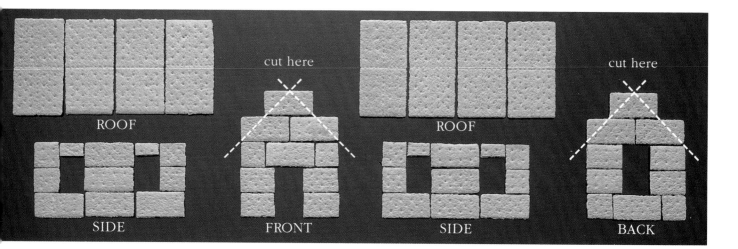

1 Cut graham crackers for the cottage to size with knife, using the pattern opposite as a guide.

2 Melt white candy coating on stove top or in microwave oven as on page 103. Spoon the coating into 1 qt. (1 L) sealable freezer bag. Squeeze coating to one corner of the bag; seal bag. Snip end from corner of bag with scissors to form writing tip.

3 Arrange ten whole graham crackers on wax-paper-lined baking sheet to make base for the cottage; space graham crackers 1/8" (3 mm) apart in two rows of five. Pipe mortar between graham crackers; press together slightly. Let base stand until set; set aside.

4 Arrange graham cracker pieces for cottage walls and roof panels on wax-paper-lined baking sheets, using pattern as a guide. Space the pieces 1/8" (3 mm) apart. Pipe mortar between pieces; press them together slightly. Let stand until set.

5 Cut peaks on the cottage walls as indicated on the pattern, using a chef's knife.

6 Decorate the roof panels with fruit-flavored gumdrop slices and mortar as shown opposite; secure with mortar. Make windows by filling interior openings on walls with hard candies. Pipe mortar around candy pieces to secure. Pipe the mortar across hard candies to make windowpanes.

7 Make shutters for windows by piping mortar over cream-filled wafer cookies, making a crosshatch design; sprinkle it with multicolored shot. Secure shutters to sides of windows with mortar. Secure pieces of licorice under the windows for flower boxes. Decorate the front wall of the cottage with candy-coated licorice pieces as shown opposite.

(Continued)

8 Place prepared graham cracker base on sheet of cardboard. Pipe mortar along lower edge of one side wall; position on the graham cracker base. Hold in place or support with heavy object until set.

9 Pipe mortar along side and base of adjoining wall, and position on base; hold in place until set. Continue to secure remaining walls to the base. Pipe additional mortar along edges where walls join. Let stand until set.

10 Make supports for the cottage roof by piping a heavy line of mortar on the inside of each roof panel, the length of supporting wall and about 1½" (3.8 cm) from lower edge of roof panel. Let stand until set.

11 Pipe mortar along upper edges of the walls. Position decorated roof panels in place, resting piped roof support along the upper edge of the walls. Let stand until set.

12 Secure roof panels by piping mortar along top of roof where the panels meet. Position the round peppermint candies along roofline, if desired; secure with mortar. Let stand until set.

13 Cut one brick from graham cracker for door, using chef's knife. For a wreath, secure hard round candy with hole in center to the door, using mortar. Tie red shoestring licorice into bow; secure to door below wreath. For the doorknob, secure silver ball to door with a dot of mortar. Let stand until set.

14 Pipe mortar along one long edge of door; secure door to the opening. Hold in place until mortar begins to set. Let stand until set. Embellish cottage with a sidewalk, icicles, shrubs, and trees, if desired (page 111).

GRAHAM CRACKER GENERAL STORE

MATERIALS

- Twenty-eight whole graham crackers.
- 1½ lbs. (750 g) white candy coating.
- 1-qt. (1 L) sealable freezer bags.
- Multicolored candy-coated licorice pieces.
- 2½" (6.5 cm) cream-filled wafer cookies.
- Multicolored hard candies.
- Small candy canes.
- Large candy cane.
- Round peppermint candies.
- Sugar cubes.
- Gumdrop wreaths.
- Small multicolored gumdrops.
- Large multicolored gumdrops.
- Red cinnamon candies.
- Multicolored fruit-flavored gumdrop slices.
- Multicolored shot.
- Sturdy cardboard.
- Wax paper.
- Baking sheet.
- 8" (20.5 cm) chef's knife.
- Assorted additional embellishments, such as red hard candies with hole in center, red shoestring licorice, silver balls, chocolate sandwich cookie, and fruit-flavored bite-size candies.

PATTERN FOR A GRAHAM CRACKER GENERAL STORE

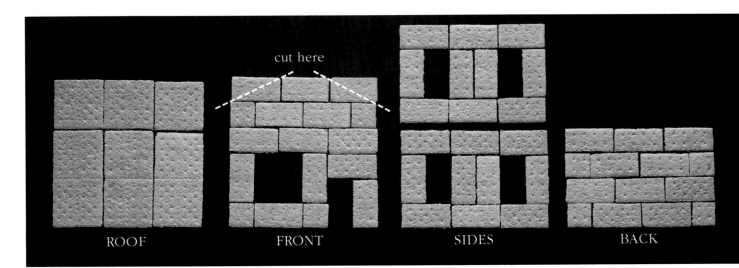

cut here

ROOF   FRONT   SIDES   BACK

1 Construct walls and roof for general store as on page 105, steps 1 to 5; use the pattern (page 107) as a guide. Spread mortar in even layer over top of assembled roof; cover evenly with fruit-flavored gumdrop slices. Let stand until set. Make the windows and shutters as on page 105, steps 6 and 7, eliminating windowpanes and flower boxes.

2 Continue as on page 106, steps 8 and 9. For awning above door, coat the top of one brick with mortar; decorate it with small gumdrop halves. For awning above front window (shown on page 107), pipe mortar over cream-filled wafer cookie in crosshatch design; sprinkle it with multicolored shot. Let stand until set.

3 Pipe mortar on one long edge of door awning. Position awning above door, piped edge against wall. Support with heavy object or hold until set. To support the awning, secure a candy cane to each side. Secure window awning in place.

4 Embellish the general store with clock, store sign, and wreaths as shown on page 107. For lamppost, cut small hole in top of large gumdrop; secure gumdrop to curved end of large candy cane with mortar. Lay on side until set.

5 Stack two or three gumdrop wreaths for the lamppost base; insert the straight end of candy cane. Secure lamppost to graham cracker base, using mortar; hold in place until set.

6 Make bench by securing two cream-filled wafer cookies at right angle. For legs, secure a sugar cube to each end of bench; for arms, secure candy-coated licorice pieces. Let stand until set. Embellish general store with sidewalk and add icicles to awnings, if desired (page 111).

GRAHAM
CRACKER
CHURCH

MATERIALS

- Thirty-three whole graham crackers.
- 1 lb. (450 g) white candy coating.
- 1-qt. (1 L) sealable freezer bags.
- Multicolored candy-coated licorice pieces.
- Multicolored hard candies.
- Large multicolored gumdrops.
- Red shoestring licorice.
- Multicolored gumdrop fruit slices.
- Small candy canes.
- Multicolored shot.
- Round, flat gumdrops.
- Sturdy cardboard.
- Wax paper.
- Baking sheets.
- 8" (20.5 cm) chef's knife.

PATTERN FOR A GRAHAM CRACKER CHURCH

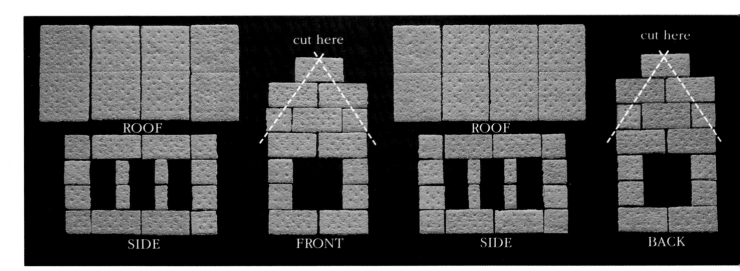

ROOF   cut here   ROOF   cut here

SIDE   FRONT   SIDE   BACK

HOW TO MAKE A GRAHAM CRACKER CHURCH

1 Construct walls and roof panels for church as on page 105, steps 1 to 5, using pattern (page 109) as a guide. Make windows by filling interior openings on back and side walls with hard candies. Pipe mortar around candy pieces to secure. Embellish church with gumdrop arches and decorate roof with mortar and multicolored shot (page 109).

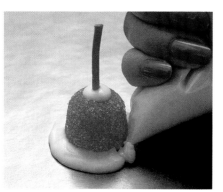

2 Continue as on page 106, steps 8 to 11, except in step 10 make roof support by piping line of mortar ½" (1.3 cm) from lower edge of roof panel. For bell, cut small hole in top of one large gumdrop; pipe small amount of mortar into hole. For the rope, insert one end of 1½" (3.8 cm) piece of shoestring licorice. Let stand until set. Pipe mortar around the bottom of the gumdrop; let stand until set.

3 Cut two whole graham crackers in half crosswise for steeple roof and walls.

4 Hold two graham cracker halves at right angle, for roof of steeple. Pipe mortar along the edge where crackers meet. Insert rope end of bell in roof seam while mortar is still wet; support with heavy object or hold in place until set. Pipe additional mortar along the roofline.

5 Secure the steeple walls to steeple roof, using mortar; hold in place until set. Pipe mortar along the lower edge of steeple walls; secure steeple to roof. Hold in place until set.

6 Make steps by overlapping four gumdrop fruit slices slightly. Secure with mortar; place round peppermint candies under steps for support. Break candy canes to desired lengths for railings; secure pieces to church and base with mortar. Hold in place until set. For doors, cut two bricks from graham crackers; embellish as desired. Secure as on page 106, step 14. Embellish church with icicles, shrubs, and village people.

TIPS FOR EMBELLISHING A GRAHAM CRACKER VILLAGE

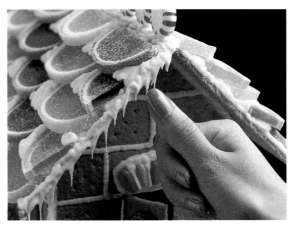

Icicles. Pipe mortar heavily along edge of the roof. Touch with thumb, and pull down slightly to form icicles. Let stand until set.

Shrubs. Break toothpicks in half. Place small gumdrops over ends of toothpicks. Insert remaining ends of toothpicks into large gumdrop, to make branches for shrub.

Trees. Melt white or chocolate-flavored candy coating as on page 103. Set the sugar cones on a wax-paper-lined baking sheet. Spoon the coating over cones; secure red cinnamon candies, popcorn, or gumdrop halves to cone. Top the tree with star cut from a flattened gumdrop, if desired.

Sidewalk. Pipe mortar strip from the front of door to the edge of base. Place hard, round peppermint candies in the mortar for stones. Fill in bare areas around stones with red cinnamon candies.

1 **Village people.** Make face from round peppermint candy; secure silver balls for eyes and small piece of shoestring licorice for mouth, using mortar. Press gumdrop through garlic press to make hair. Style the hair, and shape around face; hair will be sticky, but hardens when exposed to air.

2 Cut a sugar cone about 2" (5 cm) from pointed end, using serrated knife. Trim the pointed end slightly to flatten; discard large end. Using mortar, secure head to tip of cone. Hold in place until set.

3 Pipe mortar onto body to make clothing. Before the mortar sets, decorate it with colored sugar and multicolored shot. Pipe mortar to make arms. Flatten large gumdrops and cut small pieces to make muff and scarf.

Gift Wrapping

EMBOSSED CARDS

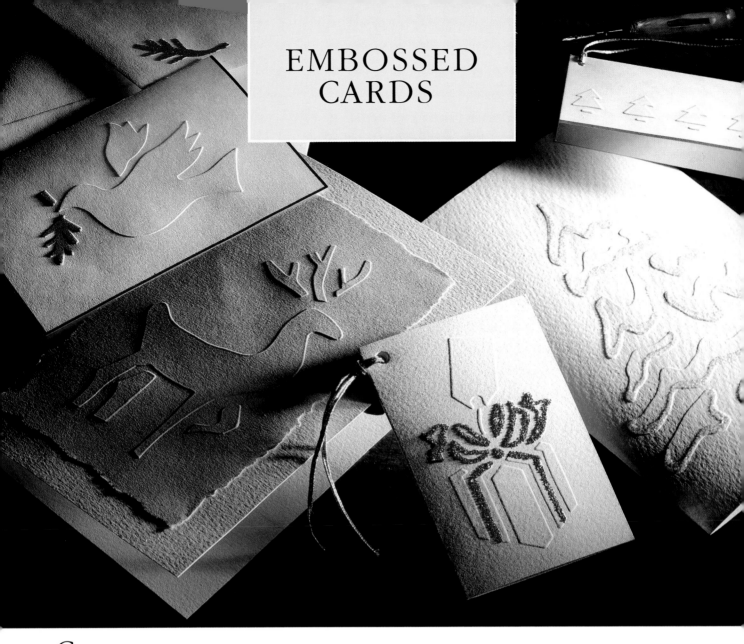

Create personalized holiday greetings by making your own embossed cards and gift tags. The embossed, or raised, design is made by placing paper over a stencil cutout and rubbing along the design with a *stylus*, a hard-pointed, pen-shaped tool. To add sparkle to the card, highlight the embossed design with glitter.

Custom stencils can be created inexpensively using transparent Mylar® sheets, available at craft stores. Designs for stencils can be found on Christmas cards or in stencil design books. Enlarge or reduce the designs, if necessary, on a photocopy machine.

Use card-stock or heavyweight stationery to prevent any tearing during embossing. Most print shops have paper, cards, and envelopes in a variety of weights and colors.

If you are cutting your own cards and tags, cut and fold the paper to the finished size before embossing. If a paper cutter is not available, use a metal straightedge, a mat knife, and a cutting mat.

When tracing around the design areas, it is necessary to place the stencil and paper over an illuminated surface,

such as a light box or a sunlit window. If the stylus has two ball ends, use the large end of the stylus for tracing around large design areas and the small end for fine, detailed areas. If the stylus squeaks as it is moved across the paper, lubricate the end by rubbing it in the palm of your hand.

MATERIALS

- Card-stock or heavyweight stationery.
- Transparent Mylar sheets.
- Fine-point permanent-ink marking pen.
- Paper cutter; or mat knife, cutting surface, such as a cutting mat, and metal straightedge.
- Stylus or small plastic crochet hook, for tracing design.
- Removable transparent tape.
- Glue pen, extra-fine glitter, and soft artist's eraser, for glittered cards.
- Light box or other illuminated glass surface.
- Cording, for gift tag.

HOW TO MAKE AN EMBOSSED CARD

1 Position Mylar® over design, allowing a 1" (2.5 cm) border; secure with tape. Trace design, using permanent-ink marking pen; simplify the shapes as necessary.

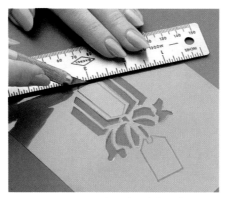

2 Cut out inner details of the design, using mat knife; use straightedge to cut along the straight lines. Cut and remove the smallest areas first, then larger ones. Pull knife toward you as you cut; turn Mylar, rather than knife, to change directions.

3 Redraw outer lines of design as necessary, to touch up any lines that were removed when cutting. Cut excess Mylar from outer edges of the design, using a mat knife and a straightedge; leave at least ¼" (6 mm) border.

4 Position the stencil as desired on front of card; secure stencil with removable tape.

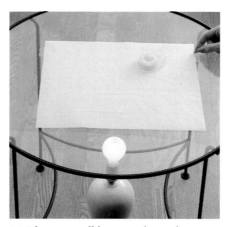

5 Place a small lamp under a glass-top table if a light box is unavailable. Tape a piece of tracing paper over the glass to act as a light diffuser, if necessary.

6 Place the card, stencil side down, on light table. Using stylus, trace outline of the design, applying firm pressure. Retrace, if necessary, for clear definition. Trace around outer edges of stencil, if desired, to frame the design.

7 Remove stencil. For glittered cards, apply glue to desired design details; sprinkle glitter over the wet glue. Shake off the excess glitter; allow glue to dry. Remove any excess glitter from card, using soft artist's eraser. Personalize card with initials, using a permanent-ink marking pen.

8 Punch hole in upper left corner of card to make gift tag. Cut 8" (20.5 cm) length of cording. Fold cording in half, and insert folded end through tag; bring the cut ends through the loop, and pull to secure.

MORE IDEAS
FOR CARDS

Gingerbread man is
cut from brown paper,
using a cookie cutter
as a pattern. The card
is embellished with
buttons, raffia, and
fabric paints in
fine-tip tubes.

Metal stars (page 29),
secured with brass
wire to a piece of
card-stock paper,
become a unique
greeting card.

Aromatic dough ornament (page 26) is glued to a piece of corrugated cardboard, to make a gift tag.

Fabric motifs are fused to a blank gift card, using paper-backed fusible web and a dry iron.

Shipping tag is used to make the gift tag above. A design is embossed onto the tag as on page 114.

Victorian cutout (left) is secured to a piece of metallic tagboard, using spray adhesive. Cut ¼" (6 mm) away from motif, and secure to card-stock paper.

STAMPED GIFT WRAPS

Make your own rubber stamps, and turn plain paper and bags into one-of-a-kind gift wraps. The stamps can also be used to embellish tissue paper and ribbons.

Stamps are made by cutting designs into artist's erasers or printing blocks, using a sharp mat knife. For easier cutting, select designs with simple details.

Stamp pads are available at art supply stores and print shops. Some metallic inks may leave oil marks on fabric ribbons. For best results, apply spray starch heavily to fabric ribbons and press them with an iron before stamping the designs.

MATERIALS

- Soft artist's eraser or printing block.
- Tracing paper.
- Transfer paper.
- Mat knife.
- Stamp pad.
- Plain wrapping paper, tissue paper, paper bags, and ribbons as desired.

HOW TO MAKE STAMPED GIFT WRAPS

1 Trace design onto paper. Transfer to smooth side of artist's eraser or printing block, using the transfer paper. Cut about ⅛" (3 mm) deep into eraser along design lines, using mat knife.

2 Remove large background area around design by cutting horizontally through the edge of eraser and up to the cuts made for the design outline.

3 Cut and remove narrow spaces within design, by cutting at an angle along each edge; remove the small background areas.

4 Press the stamp firmly onto the stamp pad; lift and repeat as necessary until the design on the stamp is evenly coated. Press stamp straight down onto paper or ribbon, using even pressure.

MORE IDEAS
FOR GIFT WRAPS

Shown left to right, top row:

Christmas message *is written across brown paper to make a personalized package.*

Organza ribbon and floral cluster *(page 100) are used as accents on a foil-wrapped package.*

Rows of jute and cotton string *are used in place of ribbon on a brown-paper package, for a natural look.*

Tea-dyed stocking ornament *is used to decorate a holiday package. The Christmas ornament becomes an extra keepsake gift.*

Shown left to right, bottom row:

Aromatic dough ornament and torn-fabric bow *are used to decorate a package, for a country look.*

Canella berries, greenery, and cones *embellish a brown-paper package that is tied with jute.*

Papier-mâché box, *shaped like a star, is embellished with pieces of imitation gold and silver leaf as on page 38. Ribbons with metallic edgings are used as an accent.*

Lace doily and organza bow *are secured to the lid of a small painted bandbox, for a romantic touch.*

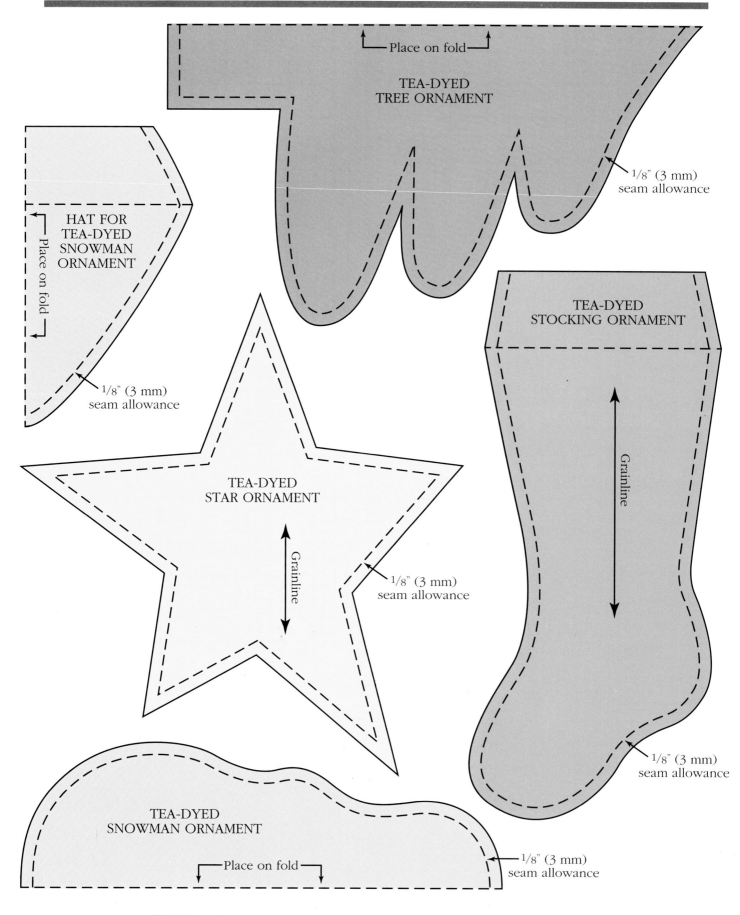

TEA-DYED
TREE ORNAMENT

Place on fold

1/8" (3 mm)
seam allowance

HAT FOR
TEA-DYED
SNOWMAN
ORNAMENT

Place on fold

1/8" (3 mm)
seam allowance

TEA-DYED
STOCKING ORNAMENT

Grainline

TEA-DYED
STAR ORNAMENT

Grainline

1/8" (3 mm)
seam allowance

1/8" (3 mm)
seam allowance

TEA-DYED
SNOWMAN ORNAMENT

Place on fold

1/8" (3 mm)
seam allowance

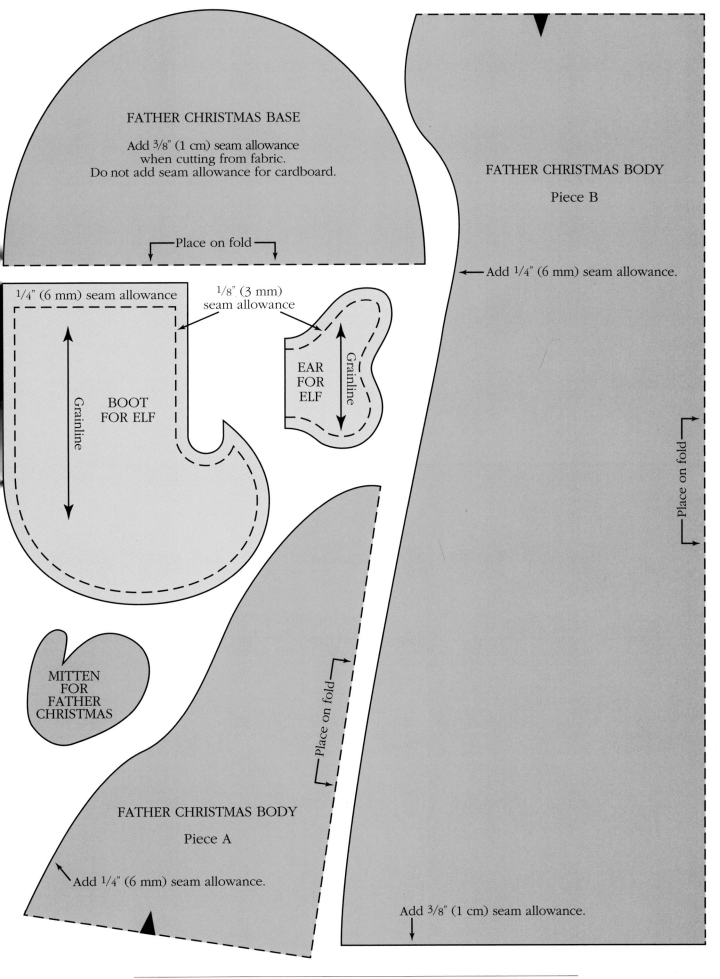

FATHER CHRISTMAS BASE

Add 3/8" (1 cm) seam allowance
when cutting from fabric.
Do not add seam allowance for cardboard.

Place on fold

FATHER CHRISTMAS BODY

Piece B

Add 1/4" (6 mm) seam allowance.

Place on fold

1/4" (6 mm) seam allowance

1/8" (3 mm)
seam allowance

Grainline

BOOT
FOR ELF

EAR
FOR
ELF

Grainline

MITTEN
FOR
FATHER
CHRISTMAS

Place on fold

FATHER CHRISTMAS BODY

Piece A

Add 1/4" (6 mm) seam allowance.

Add 3/8" (1 cm) seam allowance.

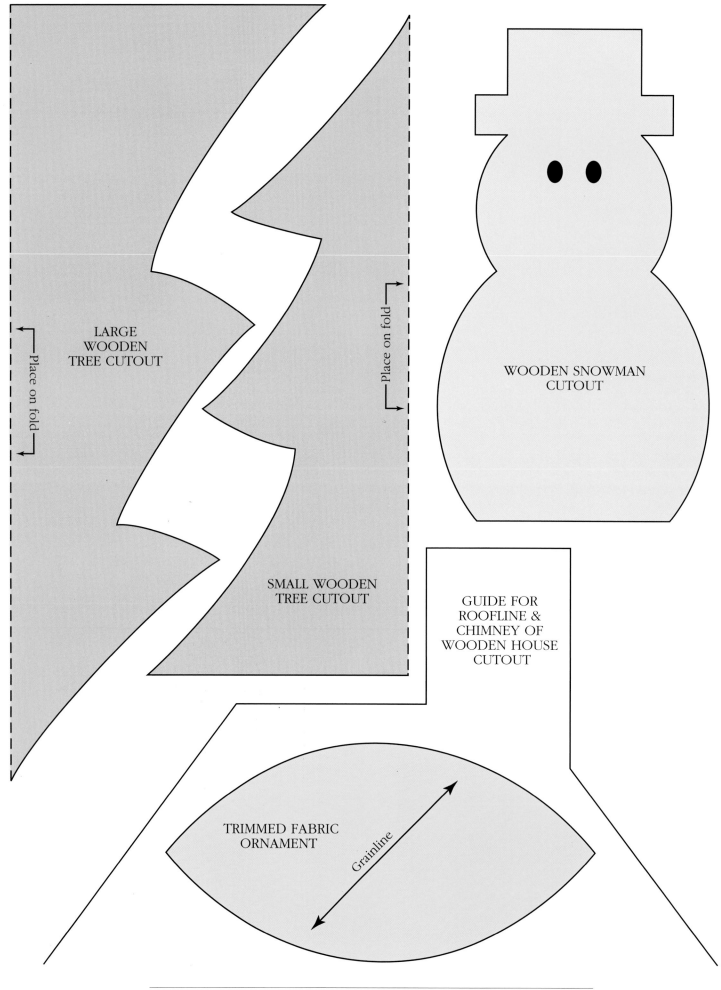

LARGE
WOODEN
TREE CUTOUT

Place on fold

Place on fold

SMALL WOODEN
TREE CUTOUT

WOODEN SNOWMAN
CUTOUT

GUIDE FOR
ROOFLINE &
CHIMNEY OF
WOODEN HOUSE
CUTOUT

TRIMMED FABRIC
ORNAMENT

Grainline

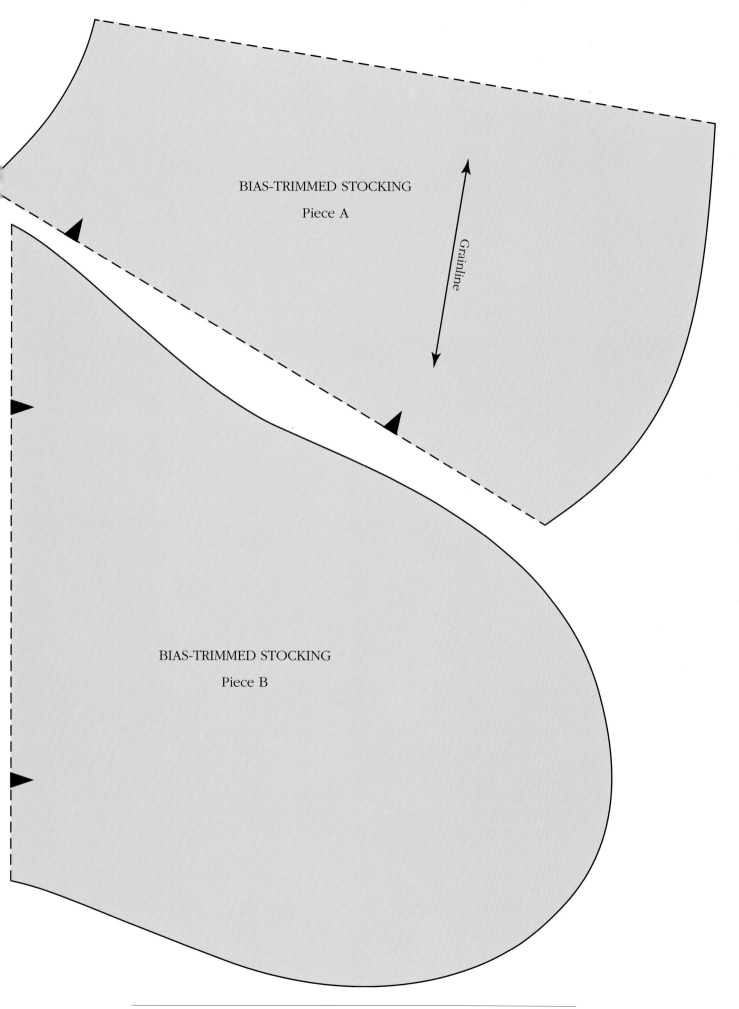

BIAS-TRIMMED STOCKING

Piece A

Grainline

BIAS-TRIMMED STOCKING

Piece B

INDEX

CY DECOSSE INCORPORATED

A COWLES MAGAZINES COMPANY

Chairman/CEO: Bruce Barnet
Chairman Emeritus: Cy DeCosse
President/COO: Nino Tarantino
Executive V.P./Editor-in-Chief:
William B. Jones

DECORATING YOUR HOME FOR
CHRISTMAS
Created by: The Editors of
Cy DeCosse Incorporated

Also available from the publisher:
*Bedroom Decorating, Creative Window
Treatments, Decorating for Christmas,
Decorating the Living Room, Creative
Accessories for the Home, Decorating
with Silk & Dried Flowers, Decorating
the Kitchen, Decorative Painting,
Kitchen & Bathroom Ideas, Decorating
for Dining & Entertaining, Decorating
with Fabric & Wallcovering, Decorating
the Bathroom*

Group Executive Editor: Zoe A. Graul
Senior Technical Director: Rita C. Arndt
Technical Director: Dawn M. Anderson
Senior Project Manager: Joseph Cella
Project Managers: Kristen Olson, Tracy
Stanley
Project Manager Intern: April Jones
Senior Art Director: Delores Swanson
Art Directors: Mark Jacobson, Linda
Schloegel
Writer: Dawn M. Anderson
Editor: Janice Cauley
Researcher/Designer: Michael Basler
Researcher: Lori Ritter
Sample Supervisor: Carol Olson
Senior Technical Photo Stylist: Bridget
Haugh
Technical Photo Stylist: Susan Pasqual
Styling Director: Bobbette Destiche
Crafts Stylist: Joanne Wawra
Assistant Crafts Stylist: Deanna Despard
Prop Assistant/Shopper: Margo Morris
Artisans: Arlene Dohrman, Sharon Eklund,
Corliss Forstrom, Phyllis Galbraith,
Kristi Kuhnau, Linda Neubauer, Carol
Pilot, Nancy Sundeen, Pat Tanner
*Vice President of Development Planning
& Production:* Jim Bindas
Director of Photography: Mike Parker
Creative Photo Coordinator: Cathleen
Shannon
Studio Manager: Marcia Chambers
Lead Photographer: Stuart Block
Photographers: Rebecca Hawthorne,

Mike Hehner, Rex Irmen, Bill Lindner,
Mark Macemon, Paul Najlis, Charles
Nields, Mike Parker, Robert Powers
Contributing Photographers: Howard
Kaplan, Paul Markert, Brad Parker
Production Managers: Laurie Gilbert,
Amelia Merz
Senior Desktop Publishing Specialist: Joe
Fahey
Production Staff: Kevin Hedden, Mike
Hehner, Robert Powers, Mike Schauer,
Kay Wethern, Nik Wogstad
Shop Supervisor: Phil Juntti
Scenic Carpenters: Rob Johnstone, John
Nadeau, Mike Peterson, Greg Wallace
Consultant: Susan Stein
Contributors: Berwick Ind.; C. M. Offray
& Son, Inc.; Concord House, Division
of Concord Fabrics Inc.; Decart Inc.;
Duncan Enterprises; Folk Art; Plaid
Enterprises; San Francisco Herb Co.;
Tolin' Station; V.I.P. Fabrics, Division
of Cranston Print Works Company;
Waverly, Division of F. Schumacher
& Co.
Printed on American paper by:
R. R. Donnelley & Sons Co. (0695)

Cy DeCosse Incorporated offers a variety
of how-to books. For information write:
Cy DeCosse Subscriber Books
5900 Green Oak Drive
Minnetonka, MN 55343